Intuition in Therapeutic Practice

Margaret Arnd-Caddigan helps clinicians to expand their understanding of intuition by introducing mind-centered dynamic therapy (MCDT), providing them with the tools to incorporate this approach into their practice.

Written accessibly for clinicians new to MCDT, the book presents this powerful method to help clients alter their thinking and overcome suffering. Divided into two parts, the book begins by clearly exploring the origins of intuition in philosophical thought, covering ideas such as panpsychism, cosmopsychism, and depth psychology views of the mind, before examining how problems arise in psychotherapy from a Relational Perspective and how MCDT can help. Chapters then demonstrate how MCDT can be used in practice by exploring specific issues and treatment implications, clearly explaining how clinicians can define and develop general intuition, what the difference between clinical intuition and intuitive inquiry is, and how clinicians can help clients develop their own intuition during sessions. Filled with practical examples, key points, and creative activities such as journaling and body work throughout, this book helps both clinicians and clients attune to and trust their own intuition in the process of healing.

Rooted in empirical research and clinical practice, this book is essential reading for counselors, psychotherapists, and clinical social workers looking to incorporate intuition into their therapeutic approach.

Margaret Arnd-Caddigan, PhD, is an associate professor of social work and a licensed clinical social worker. She is the co-author and primary researcher for *Intuition in Psychotherapy: From Research to Practice*.

"Dr. Arnd-Caddigan provides readers with a window into her method of psychotherapy, Mind-Centered Depth Therapy. This process is grounded in empirically based research and historically defined psychodynamic theories and techniques. The basis of Mind Centered Depth Therapy places it on the evolutionary ladder of psychodynamic frameworks. MCDT is organized around the construct of intuition and intuitive inquiry.

The substance of the book describes the capacity to connect psychotherapeutic relationships through the force of intuitive inquiry. The emphasis on the reality of the mind is fortified through a recognition that intuition is analogous to one of the five senses. Intuition is to appreciation and understanding of the mind as touch, taste, smell, and sight are to experiences of physical sensation.

Dr. Arnd-Caddigan makes the case for 'intuition' as a valuable data point for influencing therapeutic action. The reliance on formulaic and protocol-driven therapies defies the value of clinical wisdom derived from the inclusion of intuitive processes. Empathy as the process that enables clinicians to appreciate and understand the internal world of the client relies in part on intuition and, as stated by Dr. Arnd-Caddigan, creates the 'ability for an instance of mind to acquire information directly from another instance of mind.' The acquisition of knowledge from another requires a specific and carefully developed mode of listening. Dr. Arnd-Caddigan prompts us to listen to the internal voices that interact with the internal process of the client.

Dr. Arnd-Caddigan's work reminds clinicians that self-preparation is essential and continuous. She provides instructive advice to enhance clinicians' and clients' capacities to identify and use intuitive processes in the therapeutic dyad. This is not a self-help book, but rather a mandate to develop and use our own internal processes as clinicians. I think it is a wise inclusion to instructors of social work and psychology practice, but also is a useful book for clients to better understand the nature of therapeutic action and to be able to engage more fully in the process."

—**Marcia Spira, PhD,** *Loyola University Chicago, USA*

"In this eclectic and wide-ranging text, Margaret Arnd-Caddigan draws from the fields of psychoanalysis, analytical psychology, and philosophy of mind to offer a significant corrective to commonplace psychotherapeutic assumptions. Articulating what she terms a 'mind-centered' approach to practice, Arnd-Caddigan writes passionately of the importance that clinicians be willing to question the implicit metaphysics of Western medical discourse. Opposing biological reductionism with an emphasis on creativity and intuition, this book should be welcomed by psychotherapists looking to broaden their theoretical and clinical horizons."

—**Robin S. Brown, PhD,** *Columbia University, USA*

"It was a pleasure to read *Intuition in Therapeutic Practice: A Mind-Centered Depth Approach for Healing*. Dr. Arnd-Caddigan gracefully honors and integrates classic psychoanalytic perspectives with the sometimes elusive element of intuition. Her book provides solid theory with guidance for developing and utilizing intuition in psychotherapy, making for a stronger, more diverse approach to working with clients. Both the novice and experienced intuitive will find this book a useful addition to their clinical repertoire."

—**John Burton, EdD, LPC,** *Clinical Hypnotherapist, author of* The Sacred Sequence: Remembering the One Truth

Intuition in Therapeutic Practice

A Mind-Centered Depth Approach for Healing

MARGARET ARND-CADDIGAN

Routledge
Taylor & Francis Group

NEW YORK AND LONDON

First published 2022
by Routledge
605 Third Avenue, New York, NY 10158

and by Routledge
2 Park Square, Milton Park, Abingdon, Oxon OX14 4RN

Routledge is an imprint of the Taylor & Francis Group, an informa business

British Library Cataloguing-in-Publication Data
A catalogue record for this book is available from the British Library

Library of Congress Cataloging-in-Publication Data
Names: Arnd-Caddigan, Margaret, author.
Title: Intuition in therapeutic practice : a mind-centered depth approach
    for healing / Margaret Arnd-Caddigan.
Identifiers: LCCN 2021013246 (print) | LCCN 2021013247 (ebook) |
    ISBN 9780367548391 (hardback) | ISBN 9780367548407 (paperback) |
    ISBN 9781003090816 (ebook)
Subjects: LCSH: Intuition. | Body-mind centering. | Psychotherapy.
Classification: LCC BF315.5 .A756 2021 (print) | LCC BF315.5 (ebook) |
    DDC 153.4/4—dc23
LC record available at https://lccn.loc.gov/2021013246
LC ebook record available at https://lccn.loc.gov/2021013247

ISBN: 978-0-367-54839-1 (hbk)
ISBN: 978-0-367-54840-7 (pbk)
ISBN: 978-1-003-09081-6 (ebk)

DOI: 10.4324/9781003090816

Typeset in Dante and Avenir
by Apex CoVantage, LLC

Contents

Preface

This book is the culmination of several seemingly separate processes that coalesced at a critical moment. One significant event was my most recent research. I am an academic clinical social worker. As an academic, I teach classes and conduct practice-focused research. As a licensed clinical social worker, I practice psychotherapy. I am extremely fortunate in that I get to teach and engage in research in an area that inspires passion in me: psychotherapy. The questions that have guided my research throughout my career have been the following. What do real-live psychotherapists *actually* do? How do they make clinical decisions in the moment with their clients? How do they decide from the extremely complex narratives their clients share which thread they pick up on and explore? How does therapy contribute to change in people? In the great debate over whether psychotherapy is more an art or a science, I have found myself exploring the more creative aspects of the practice.

One of my studies focused on how therapists resolve boundary dilemmas. I was surprised to find that most of the therapists I interviewed revealed that they used their intuition or gut feeling in making the decision. The literature on ethics certainly does not support this means of decision-making. At the risk of sounding hyperbolic, this response rocked my world.

In fact, I had a history with the idea of using intuition as a clinical tool. When I was a student doing field work, my supervisor once asked me how I knew to pursue a line of inquiry with a particular client. I told him I used my intuition. He told me that there was no such thing as intuition. He insisted that there must have been something that cued me, and I needed to go back and figure out what that was.

I did what I typically do when faced with a question: I immediately bought a book on the subject. At that time, both business researchers and cognitive psychologists were beginning to study the phenomenon. While the book I read confirmed to me that intuition is "real," I also got the message loud and clear that it was not something I could talk about freely with other therapists. But when I did my research on boundaries, I got the affirmation I had waited years to receive. I pretty quickly designed a study on clinical intuition. My co-author and I wrote up the results in *Clinical Intuition: From Research to Practice*.

Running through all of my work is my love of Relational Psychoanalytic Thought. My doctoral degree program was heavily psychoanalytically focused. I was able to narrow that focus to the Relational Schools in my electives and dissertation. I use the plural for Relational Schools as a shorthand for a few different strands of contemporary analytic thought that frequently intertwine. In using the term, I am referring to the Relational Work Proper (including such thinkers as Steven Mitchell, Lewis Aron, etc.), the Interpersonal School (beginning with H. S. Sullivan and including such figures as Donnel Stern), and the analysts who study from an Intersubjective Perspective (including such thinkers as Robert Stolorow, George Atwood, etc.). One reviewer for the book proposal I first submitted to Routledge stated that there is nothing new in the text. I think this is basically right (although I believe I put things together in a novel way). I have been studying and practicing from a Relational Psychoanalytic Perspective for decades. It is so deeply engrained in my perspective that I cannot see things otherwise.

My relationship to Jungian thought is a bit more complicated. I was introduced to analytical psychology when I was a student studying the history of religions. I took a course in the psychology of religion wherein we studied Jung. I closely studied the works of Mircea Eliade and his protégé, my advisor, Ion Couliano, in an attempt to better understand the relationship between "magic"/the occult and religions. This work included a good bit of Jungian thought. I left that program before I finished my doctorate, due to Dr. Couliano's tragic death. I decided to become a psychotherapist.

In my two degrees in social work, Jung was barely mentioned. My master's program did not have a clinical emphasis. During that experience, I was taught that I needed to put my ideas about religion and spirituality (and definitely about magic) on a back burner in order to practice ethically. My doctorate, which was clinically focused, was very psychoanalytic. It is not uncommon for psychoanalytic-focused programs to omit Jungian thought. So, what I learned about Jung—archetypes, alchemy, and the like—in my first doctoral program kind of hung around in the back of mind. It certainly influenced my worldview and thus how I conducted psychotherapy, but it did not show up in my academic publications.

It was not until I came upon the Transpersonal psychologists, when I was designing the research that informed *Clinical Intuition: From Research to Practice*, that I decided to re-visit Jungian thought. At that point, my literature review included Jung, Jungians, and post-Jungians. But perhaps the most striking experience was when I read 39 transcripts of podcasts by David Van Nuys (www.ShrinkRapRadio.com). "Dr. Dave" has interviewed noted Jungian analysts and scholars as well as post-Jungians in a host of disciplines. It seemed to me from this material that under the title of "Jungian," there is room for a good bit of heterogeneity in thought. And many of the thinkers were articulating perspectives that were consistent with the worldview that I held. Perhaps I was actually more Jungian (or post-Jungian) than I suspected. And having said that, it is still clear that the theory I advance in this book differs from analytical psychology in some important ways.

I feel that I must also add that while I studied religions, and while many Jungians and post-Jungians use his work to pursue spiritual ends, I am a psychotherapist. Most of my clients come to me with a commitment to a religious path. They are not seeking a therapist to act as a guide on a spiritual journey. They are looking to me to help them with worldly problems in living. Thus, in working out a mind-centered depth therapy (MCDT), even though I find it essential to be clear on the worldview out of which the theory and practice arise, the therapy itself is suited to helping clients with mundane matters.

The mind-body relationship has also been an enduring part of my work. I began my career learning about the stress response, biofeedback, and reading a great deal of psycho-neuro-immunology and affective neuroscience. I, like so many other therapists, did not reflect on the philosophical underpinnings of this approach to therapy. I knew that mind and body were connected, not two separate things. But I failed to understand that many of the people who were writing about the connection were implying that mind was a side effect of the brain or neurochemical processes. Over time, I began to see more and more that people were trying to help those who were suffering mentally overcome their pain by manipulating the body. This just seemed really off to me.

So, intuition is real and legitimate. And there was something about the mind-body conversation and approach to psychotherapy that was hitting me wrong. It all came together for me when I read an article on panpsychism. There was a group of very smart people—not "woo-woo" or new-agey types, but serious philosophers—who were suggesting that mind was real, and was not an epiphenomenon of the brain. It immediately struck me that the implications of this perspective were tremendous for psychotherapy, intuition, and using intuition as an important clinical tool. It became very clear to me that if I re-cast my beloved psychoanalytic theory through the lens of a branch of panpsychism-cosmopsychism, then I could openly discuss how and why intuition is at the very heart of my work. As it turns out, the result is highly consistent with what many contemporary Jungians and post-Jungians propose.

And, as sometimes occurs, it appears that good ideas occur to unrelated people. Shortly after I published an article (Arnd-Caddigan, 2019) in which I advocated for a dual aspect ontology (a worldview that holds both mind and matter to be equally real and fundamental) in psychotherapy, Robin Brown (2020) published a book in which he advocated for the blending of psychoanalytic and analytical psychology with panpsychism. This kind of synchronicity serves to confirm my belief that the time is ripe to develop these ideas.

I began to practice from my coalescing perspective. I began using insights and finding that clients responded very well. I began telling my students, supervisees, and colleagues about what I was understanding, and they all seemed to think it had merit.

There is another contributing factor to the final form this book has taken. I conceptualized this book in the summer of 2019. I obtained a contract from Routledge on March 26, 2020, as we in the United States (US) were becoming painfully aware of the seriousness of the Covid-19 pandemic. Soon thereafter, on May 25, George Floyd was killed. I finished the first draft of this book a few weeks before the 2020 election in the US. The campaigning for this election—which stretched from the primaries that began in February to the final national election in November—was quite painful for many in the US.

So there I was, sequestered in my house, aware of how privileged I was to be able to continue my jobs teaching and conducting therapy via video communication. Also, I was feeling the frustration and enervation that video communication creates. The danger of the contagion of Covid-19 emphasized for me the degree of connectedness between people. We all became highly aware of the fact that our physical connection is such that we exchange bodily fluids at six feet. If that is the degree of our physical connection, bounded as it is by time and space, how much more connected must our minds be? Yet the concomitant social unrest highlighted the degree to which we are still all unique. As connected as we are, there are important differences that should never be overlooked or devalued.

That which makes us unique makes us each precious to the same degree as our connection makes each of us instrumental to the well-being of the whole. We cannot live this truth joyously if we continue believing that the only things that are important in the world are that which we can count.

Doing so has wrought a mental health crisis, an environmental crisis, and a social crisis. We have "lost our minds," and we must re-mind ourselves of who we are and what is important in order for our species to survive. It is my hope that we celebrate our dual aspects of mind and body, separateness and connectedness, and that helping clients to do so allows them to feel truly at home as "themselves," as they embrace the role they play in the health of the whole.

I must acknowledge the help of colleagues in creating this work. Rachel Harris, Karen Silinsky, and Louise Hudak were generous in reviewing early drafts and offering valuable suggestions. The personnel at Routledge, especially my editor Heather Evans, were equally generous in their help in bringing this book into being. The continual support of the Greenville Psychoanalytic Study Group has been a bedrock for all of my work. Finally, there is my family. Without their support, encouragement, and faith in me, I could not have accomplished any of my successes.

References

Arnd-Caddigan, M. (2019). Clinical intuition and the non-material: An argument for dual-aspect monism. *Journal of Religion and Spirituality in Social Work: Social Context, 38*(3), 281–295. https://doi.org/10.1080/15426432.2019.1626318

Brown, R. S. (2020). *Groundwork for a transpersonal psychoanalysis: Spirituality, relationship, and participation.* Routledge.

Introduction: A Mind-Centered Depth Approach

This is a book about how I do psychotherapy. The way I refer to my approach is as a mind-centered depth therapy (MCDT). I use lower case letters here because I do not see this as a separate "brand" of psychotherapy but rather as an approach. I use the letters MCDT as a shorthand. As the title of this book implies, it is a highly intuitive approach to the treatment of mental suffering. You may have picked up the book because of the word "intuitive" in the title; after all, this is not a way of doing therapy that has gotten a lot of attention. The book explains how and why intuition is an appropriate approach to psychotherapy. The gist is this: just as measuring things is a good way to know more about the physical world, intuition is the way that we know the mental aspects of the world. Intuition gives us insight into others' minds, and it also helps us understand our own mind better. Thus, intuition is the primary tool we use in MCDT. Let's break down the components of the term MCDT as a way to introduce this way of working.

First, let's look at the term "depth." Depth psychologies are those approaches to psychotherapy that work on the level of the unconscious. This includes the psychoanalytic schools and analytical psychology. The psychoanalytic schools are those approaches to psychoanalysis and psychotherapy that can trace a lineage to Sigmund Freud. I am most aligned with the Relational branch of the Freudian tree. Analytical psychology is the approach to analysis and psychotherapy that traces its lineage to Carl Jung and includes post-Jungians that support diverse perspectives.

Some people reading this book may have a lot of experience with psychoanalytic thought and/or analytical psychology. My guess is, many of you

DOI: 10.4324/9781003090816-1

have not. My experience in academia has taught me that most students have learned three things about psychoanalytic thought: they have learned some limited Freudian theory (like drive theory), they have learned that psychoanalytic practice died some time around the middle of the last century, and they have learned that it is not an evidence-based practice. They may have learned that Jung broke from Freud and developed the ideas of the collective unconscious and archetypes, with little understanding of what these concepts actually mean.

While Freud and Jung really did come up with the theories you may have learned in school, you may be surprised to learn that neither theoretical approach has died. In fact, both have evolved and continue to do so. For example, many contemporary analysts no longer endorse key aspects of Freudian theory, most notably his drive theory.

A Brief History of Depth Psychologies

As I have indicated, depth psychologies consist of the Freudian (psychoanalytic) and Jungian (analytical psychology) branches. Both are considered depth psychologies because the practitioners work at the level of the unconscious. Sigmund Freud is the father of psychoanalysis. He was first introduced to "the talking cure" by the physician Josef Breuer in the 1880s. From that point forward, Freud developed a series of theories on how the human psyche works. This includes both normal and pathological development, along with a theory and techniques for how to cure pathological conditions. Freud accrued a number of students and colleagues who formed the Vienna Psychoanalytic Society. This society, with Freud at its head, held authority over the ideas and perspectives that were acknowledged as "psychoanalytic." As divergent ideas arose, the originators of those ideas left the psychoanalytic society and developed alternatives to Freudian psychoanalysis.

Carl Jung was one such thinker. Jung was already a noted psychiatrist when he joined up with Freud and become the latter's disciple. Over time. he differed with his mentor to the degree that Freud no longer considered him to be a representative of psychoanalysis. As happened with other apostates, Jung continued his work distinct from the Freudian aegis. Most notably, it was Jung's elaboration on the theory of the unconscious that triggered his break from Freud. Jung accrued his own students, all of whom continued to develop Jung's theories. Because Jung left the Freudian circle early, his work is often overlooked by most analysts who consider themselves to belong in the Freudian lineage. Although, it must be immediately noted that this is changing today. There is more and more call for rapprochement between the two forms of analysis.

After Freud's death, his students continued to elaborate on his work. Disagreements and differences continued to emerge. Except now, rather than being expelled from the analytic society, some of the originators of these differences remained under the psychoanalytic umbrella. They became representatives of different schools within Freudian psychoanalysis. One of these schools was the British Object Relations School. The focus of this school was on how real relationships very early in life continue to influence the way an individual experiences themselves and others, and sets an expectation for how relationships should operate.

In the 1950s, an American psychiatrist, Harry Stack Sullivan, was interested in the theory and treatment of psychiatric disorders but rejected psychoanalytic theory (later, one of his close associates underwent analytic training and there was some unification of the approaches). Sullivan developed a system of understanding and treating what he termed "problems in living." This system is known as Interpersonal Psychoanalysis. Interpersonal Psychoanalysis is based on the notion that there is no such thing as an individual mind. Rather, all psychological functioning can only be understood as emerging from an interpersonal context. One must understand that context in order to help people change.

In the 1980s, members of the British Object Relations School of Analysis and Interpersonal Psychoanalysts began working together based on similarities in the theories. They called their new school of psychoanalysis Relational Psychoanalysis. At about the same time, analysts Robert Stolorow and George Atwood advanced an Intersubjective Approach to analysis, which had a good deal of overlap with the Relational Theories that were evolving. This approach was that human development and psychotherapy were not understandable in terms of a single mind. Minds must be connected in order for growth or healing to take place. I use material written by analysts who identify as relational, interpersonal, and intersubjective under the umbrella term "Relational Psychoanalysis."

Just as Freud's followers developed his theories after his death, Jung's did as well. Today, the term "post-Jungian" very loosely applies to perspectives that are rooted in Jungian concepts. While much of the work focuses on psychotherapy, this is not a necessary condition to be post-Jungian. Some noted post-Jungians are much more focused on spirituality. Specifically, the Transpersonal psychologists, who acknowledge their use of Jungian thought, have developed ideas that are consistent with the worldview that informs MCDT.

Evidence-Based Practice

We saw previously that the notion that psychoanalysis died in the twentieth century is not accurate. As for the belief that psychoanalysis and psychodynamic psychotherapy are not evidence-based practices, that is also not true. When it was first announced that psychoanalytic practice was not an evidence-based practice, what this meant was that there was not a body of outcome studies and meta-analyses of outcome studies to prove that it worked. This is not the same as saying that there's proof it doesn't work. It just means that those particular kinds of research had not been used to investigate psychoanalytic therapy thus far.

A group of dedicated researchers and statisticians took up the challenge and set out to study psychoanalytic practice using the gold standards of evidence-based practice, and they found that this form of treatment is highly effective in a number of domains, including symptom reduction and general levels of well-being. I highly recommend you consult the website of Jonathan Shedler (www.jonathanshedler.com) if you are interested in learning about some of these findings. But the reason psychoanalytic practitioners were late to the game in terms of evidence-based practice is that many of them have had a similar experience as I had: outcome studies and meta-analyses never really helped me figure out what to do with a specific client in order to help them. There remains today some ambivalence about the concept of evidence-based practice among psychoanalysts and psychodynamic psychotherapists.

I have been a psychodynamic psychotherapist for decades. I have studied psychoanalytic theory for decades. Any form of therapy I may conduct must, on the basis of my experience and proclivities, be premised on a strong psychoanalytic foundation. Those of you who are familiar with psychoanalytic thought will appreciate just how dependent I am on the works of those analysts who have influenced my therapy practices throughout my career. And you will note that I diverge from this foundation in some important ways. Those of you who are not familiar with psychoanalytic thought may be relieved to learn that you will not have to study this approach to treatment for decades as I have in order to be able to conduct mind-centered depth psychotherapy. But if this book spurs you to further investigate this rich body of literature, and/or the work of Jung, the Jungians, and the post-Jungians, I will consider that a plus.

Mind-Centered

There has been a growing consensus that the mind and the body cannot be separated. It has been a bit disconcerting to see that among many of the advocates for mind-body approaches to therapy, the central focus is the body. In reading the work of several philosophers of mind, it became clear to me that mind-body approaches to therapy are based on materialism—the view that what is "real" is limited to that which has physical properties. Anything that does not exist in space—meaning it does not have mass, volume, density, etc.—either does not exist or can be understood as an epiphenomenon of physical processes. From this perspective, because mind does not have physical properties, either minds don't actually exist or they are a side effect of neurochemical processes (located mainly, but not exclusively, in the brain). From this perspective, the way to change the mind is to alter the brain/body.

This was indeed the hope of psychiatry since the turn of the twentieth century. As carefully documented by Robert Whitaker (2010/2015, 2019), medical practitioners have long sought to understand mental suffering as a disease of the brain and to treat it by altering the sufferer's biology. This tendency has perhaps been re-fueled by the advances in neuroscience, which seeks to demonstrate the correlation between changes in the brain structure and functioning and subjective experience.

But this agenda has been challenged by philosophers of science. There are a growing number of such scholars who question the underlying principle of the "medical model." They have suggested that the mind is not a side effect of the body but is instead a very real, fundamental aspect of the universe.

A mind-centered depth approach to psychotherapy is premised on the idea that the mind is real and not an epiphenomenon of neurochemical processes. Indeed, given that the mind has no physical properties, it is not best understood using the same methods as one uses to know the physical aspects of the universe. Just as we use our five senses, measurements, and statistics to learn about the physical aspects of the universe, we use intuition to know about the mind.

The Logic of the Text

This book is divided into two parts. The first four chapters are highly theoretical. I begin with the premise that what you think about the nature of the world is going to highly affect how you live in it. Whether you articulate your understanding on an overt level or if it lurks under the surface, it nonetheless exerts an implicit force. I think that being explicit about it puts us in a better position to make choices. I also think that what you think about the human condition is going to influence your attempt to help ease the suffering of others. Again, I am clear that being aware of your position puts you in a better position to act purposefully. It's very hard to figure out what you're going to do in the moment with a unique client if you don't have a clear idea about what might be accomplished, and how it is that people change.

Not only do I value a clear understanding regarding an approach to therapy, but I am also acutely aware of the valence of the word intuition in our culture. At a time when some people want therapy to be scientifically based, suggesting that we proceed intuitively may cause some consternation. If I'm going to advocate for using intuition as the primary tool in psychotherapy, I feel as though I need to offer an explanation that is coherent and cohesive for why and how it is a legitimate approach.

For those of you who are not interested in theory, the good news is that the second part of the book is comprised of concrete recommendations for practicing from a mind-centered depth approach. These chapters outline what intuition is and how to develop it for use both in your life as well as in your clinical practice. I also suggest that teaching your clients to develop and trust their own intuition might be clinically helpful.

The argument of this book unfolds in the following way. In the first chapter, I review the relevant work on panpsychism and cosmopsychism. This is the philosophical position that both mind and matter are fundamental aspects of the universe. This means that both are real and neither one is reducible to the other. Because they are aspects of a single universe, they are correlated. If you change one, the other will change, but this is not due to causation.

Cosmopsychism is the branch of panpsychism in which it is asserted that the universe itself is a whole. Rather than being comprised of smaller and smaller units that coalesce to create this whole, the whole is fundamental. Smaller units within that whole are grounded by subsumption in the singularity. The chapter unpacks the implications of this view for what mind is.

The next chapter explores what mind is from the perspective of the Relational Schools within psychoanalytic theory and analytical psychology. It will become clear that re-casting the analytic views of the mind into cosmopsychist terms requires a slight alteration, but it is not a huge jump. There are in fact many similarities in the views, certainly enough to justify the interpretive leap.

Chapter 3 explores how the Relational Psychoanalytic Schools view the causes for psychological suffering, and how the Jungian perspective on this issue is quite consistent with this view. I lay out the argument among Relational Analysts regarding how analytic therapy helps clients feel better. I then show how filtering these theories and practices through the cosmopsychist lens creates the theoretical basis of MCDT.

The fourth chapter is on the twin senses of self and how these arise out of the experiences of the sources of qualia, or experiences (which, we will see, is what the mind is). Psychoanalytic theory stresses the need to experience the self as an autonomous, bounded, unique individual, and the goal of Jungian therapy is to individuate—to become more of the self. They both blinker the benefits of also experiencing the self as a connected and permeable part of the whole. The post-Jungian Transpersonal therapists offer an alternative to this one-sided view of the self, stressing the benefits of understanding the self as connected to the Transpersonal source. In MCDT, the therapist helps the client balance both experiences of the self.

The first four chapters constitute the theoretical part of the book. In this first part, intuition is mentioned several times, but it is not elaborated on. The second part of the book is about the practice of MCDT, which is centered on both the therapist's use of their intuition as well as teaching clients to use and trust their own intuition. Chapter 5 lays out a definition of intuition. The next chapter suggests methods you can use to enhance your own intuition in a general way. Chapter 7 offers suggestions for using your intuition in the clinical context, and how this differs from general intuition due to the professional relationship. Chapter 8 offers some insight into how and why you might consider helping your client learn to access and trust their own intuitive capacities.

If you are not familiar with the depth psychologies, you may be surprised (or even dismayed) that I do not directly address symptoms of explicit mental health diagnoses in this book. From the analytic perspective, such diagnoses are themselves symptoms. From the perspective of MCDT, they are qualia. As qualia are an important focus of this way of approaching psychotherapy, symptoms and mental illness are indeed central concerns. But they are far from the only concern, and usually aren't even the primary concern. The source of the qualia and the way the experiences impact the sense of self as an individual and the sense of self as connected to others and the whole is believed to have a more profound impact on one's overall functioning and well-being. Thus, as is the case with the analytic psychotherapies, symptom reduction may be an objective that will help us reach the ultimate goal of well-being through enhanced flexibility in the kinds of experiences that one is capable of having. But it is not the ultimate goal of therapy.

MCDT is an approach to psychotherapy that holds intuition at the very heart of treatment. This includes both the therapist's intuition as well as that of the client. While some might easily dismiss the approach as illegitimate, it is in fact supported by meta-theoretical and theoretical justification from philosophy and analytic thought. It is my sincere hope that for those of you who have been secretly practicing this way, this book will validate and help you take pride in your work. For those of you who have wondered if your intuition could be used in therapy, I hope this book gives you some tips for how to do so. For those of you who have not considered the value of intuition in psychotherapy, this book may offer an argument that may give you something to think about. Perhaps it may expand your possibilities.

References

Whitaker, R. (2010/2015). *Anatomy of an epidemic: Magic bullets, psychiatric drugs, and the astonishing rise of mental illness in America.* Broadway Books.

Whitaker, R. (2019). *Mad in America: Bad science, bad medicine, and the enduring mistreatment of the mentally ill.* Basic Books.

Part I
A Philosophy of Mind

Panpsychism and Cosmopsychism

1

I am a psychotherapist. I conduct treatment (therapy) for mind (psyche). In order to do this, I think it's very important to have some idea about the nature of the mind. The way that we understand mind is based on our worldview. In psychotherapy, techniques come from theory, and theory comes from worldview (also called meta-theory or paradigm). Our meta-theory has two parts: ontology and epistemology. The words refer to the way that we understand fundamental questions about the world. Our ontology, or ontological position, is the way we answer the question what is the nature of reality? What is real; what is the fundamental nature of reality? Our epistemological perspective is the way we answer the questions how do we know about the world? How do we acquire knowledge? What is legitimate knowledge?

The treatment part of psychotherapy is aimed at helping our clients change. The way we understand the reality of the mind is going to highly influence what, exactly, we are targeting for change, and how we go about trying to change that. How do we know what specific kinds of changes to the mind might be helpful to a specific client? Each theory of psychotherapy and psychological counseling has an implicit or explicit view on these questions.

Panpsychism is an ontology that has roots that extend as far back as ancient Greek philosophy. Recently, this view of reality has been gaining support by some contemporary philosophers of mind. There are many areas of disagreement among philosophers who identify as panpsychists. Each of these differences can impact the way we think about therapy and, thus, what we do in our practice. One of the positions some panpsychist philosophers take is cosmopsychism. This view will be explored in detail. As will become clear, the implications for psychotherapy are profound.

DOI: 10.4324/9781003090816-3

The view of mind offered by panpsychism and cosmopsychism may be enhanced by another movement in the philosophy of mind. This is the extended mind theory. Taking these two views of mind into consideration, the resulting conclusion is that our minds exist beyond our bodies, and can connect. This suggests an epistemology for psychotherapy. How do we know about our clients' minds, their mental processes and contents? It is possible that another's mind can be known directly through connection. As a result of the connection, both minds expand to admit new experience.

This ability to share experience is at the very heart of clinical intuition, and forms the epistemological position of MCDT. Clinical intuition has been shown to be a powerful tool that therapists from different theoretical backgrounds rely on in order to help people improve their mental functioning. MCDT is designed from the epistemological position that minds can directly influence and experience each other.

1.1 The Definitions of Matter and Mind in Panpsychism

Before we look at the philosophy of mind that guides the therapy set forward in this book, we have to be clear about what we mean by matter and mind. Most people are probably very comfortable with their understanding of matter, or things that physically exist. We know a great deal about matter; we have been learning about it since we were in grade school. For example, we know that it exists in space; it has properties like mass, volume, and density. That is, we can measure it. We know that we can perceive matter with our senses: it possesses texture, smell, or color, etc. This is all probably pretty well understood by most readers.

But when it comes to the nature of mind, there is less clarity. There are different definitions of mind. For example, some psychologists have defined mind as,

> an incredibly complex set of interactive cognitive processes, which includes analyzing, comparing, evaluating, planning, remembering, visualizing, and so on. And all of these complex processes rely on the sophisticated system of symbols we call human language.
>
> (Harris, 2019, p. 19)

This quote suggests that mind is our rational, discursive, analytic thinking processes. Mind is something that we are capable of reflecting on. And mind is related to our ability to generate and manipulate symbols. The most important symbol from this perspective is language: the way we use words to represent our experiences. By stating that mind is language, the role of culture becomes very important: language reflects the categories that are culturally endorsed. For example, in Western culture, we used to only be able to see gender as binary. This blinded people to an array of other gender experiences. The epistemology implicit in this definition of mind is that the way we can know about our clients' minds is through the words they share with us. This further implies that we can only know what the client is aware of, or able to reflect on and talk about.

Panpsychist philosophers have a very different definition of mind. They define mind as "what-it's-likeness." Mind, or phenomenal consciousness,

> is a general property that comes in specific forms: pain, anxiety, and the forms of experience involved in seeing red, or smelling gasoline, or tasting coffee. Specific forms of phenomenal consciousness are variously called *conscious states, experiential properties, or phenomenal properties*. . . . how . . . [experiences] feel or what it's like to have them, are known as 'phenomenal concepts.'
>
> (Goff, 2017, p. 3)

The term "qualia" (singular, "quale") is often used to denote this qualitative nature of mind. These are experiences that cannot be communicated by describing physical processes. For example, "My muscles are tensed up and squeezing on a nerve" does not capture the pain that I am experiencing. Such experiences are, contrary to the previous definition, often difficult to put into words or directly designate. Perhaps the most important example of mindedness, from a psychotherapeutic perspective, is what it's like to be "me." There are sub-sets of this experience, as in what it's like to feel sad and tired and anhedonia all at once, or what it's like to have had my partner just tell me that they are leaving me.

Mind includes not only the aspect of qualia but also the subjective experience that the qualia are happening to "me" (Benovsky, 2018). Thus, the sense of self becomes a central issue in a mind-centered therapy. This will be explored in greater detail in Chapter 4. What is important to stress here is that mind, by definition, is tied to a sense of self.

1.2 Is Mind Real?

Freud's work was historically situated at a time when the dominant worldview was Logical Positivism. This view was based on the ontology known as materialism or physicalism. The ontology posits that reality is made up of matter: that is, reality was held to be limited to that which has physical properties. This is where we get the statement we all learned in graduate school: "If you can't count it, it isn't real."

Given this belief (the position can't be proven by any means that does not come from research that is based on the very position it seeks to prove), when Freud set about to study mind it should not be surprising that he framed his theory in the language of physicality: he represented both his topographic model (the conscious, the preconscious, and the unconscious) and structural model (id, ego, and superego) of mind as existing in space and having structure. Greenberg and Mitchell (1983) emphasized this point in their discussion of Freud's drive / structure model:

> Freud implied at times that drive is to be understood as a quasi-physiological quantity, which exercises force mechanistically within the mind. The express intention of the *Project for a Scientific Psychology* (1895a) was to establish psychology on the same materialistic basis as that which supported other natural sciences. . . . He often expressed the hope that his hypothesized psychic structures would someday be confirmed by anatomical finding, and his attempts to create a pictorial representation of the mental apparatus (1923a, 1933) indicate that he thought of the mind as existing in physical space.
>
> (Greenberg & Mitchell, 1983, pp. 21–22)

It is little wonder that over time when many analytic thinkers and other psychotherapists discussed mind, its parts and operations, they spoke of it as if it were a thing. Many non-analytic therapists decided to ignore mind altogether: they decided that they would only focus on things that they could count, like observable behaviors, or clients' reports (words) of specific thoughts.

This position has changed over time. In particular, the Interpersonal, Relational, and Intersubjective Psychoanalytic Theorists discuss the process of how mind structures experience, as opposed to the mind being or having a structure (Mitchell, 1988). And yet, there continues to be a pull toward materialism that is evident in the widespread adoption of neuroscience as an explanation for mental processes. From this perspective, the physical—biological neurochemical processes—that occur in the body are believed to cause mental functions. The good news here is that it is acceptable to talk about mind again. Suddenly, psychotherapy is viewed as a bit more legitimate.

But this legitimacy comes at a price. By making all experiences ultimately neurochemical, we blinker the centrality of subjectivity in humanity. Nearly all humans have a direct experience of their minds. As Goff (2019a) noted, one's mind is the only aspect of reality of which one has a direct experience; all other experiences, including our experiences of our bodies and the physical world, are mediated by our minds!

While seeing the mind as a by-product of the brain (or neurochemical processes that are located throughout the entire body) may have helped psychotherapists achieve a degree of respectability, the view itself is the product of the mind. For this and other reasons, philosophers of mind have arrived at the position that mind is not based on biological processes. They call their perspective "panpsychism." Most simply put, panpsychism is the position that mind and matter are both fundamental and omnipresent in the universe. Both are fundamental, meaning that mind is not reducible to matter. Matter does not cause, create, or gives rise to mind. Of particular interest in this context is the point that mind is not a side effect of neurochemical processes. Put more bluntly, the mind is not the brain. Thus, panpsychism is the position that mind (in more complex forms, consciousness) is as real as matter.

If mind and matter are both real, the question may arise as to what, exactly, they have to do with each other. Early philosophers suggested that mind and matter were entirely distinct: they represented separate realities: "There are, under dualism, two 'ontological realms', the mental and the physical, and they both are—ontologically speaking—autonomous" (Benovsky, 2018, p. 11). From this perspective, it is difficult to understand how the human mind and body can have an effect on each other, or why changes in one are so closely correlated to changes in the other. Yet we know that your body and your mind *do* affect each other. Mind and matter are highly correlated in humans. But as we were continually reminded in graduate school, correlation is not causation. A panpsychist position is that mind and matter are correlated because they are both aspects of a single reality: a single universe.

Two panpsychist philosophers, Godehard Bruntrup (2017), along with Jiri Benovsky (2018) identified panpsychism with dual aspect monism as an alternative to strict dualism. That is, it is a "one-category ontology . . . [in which] there is only one kind of thing but it features physical and mental properties" (Bruntrup, p. 51). Benovsky used the term "phental"—both physical and mental—to designate the singularity of reality. This position solves the problem as to why they are so tightly correlated: one cannot heat up the head of coin without the tail becoming warmer. Thus, if one's mind changes, we would expect there to be some change in physical properties, as well. This does not mean that the change in the mind is caused by the alteration in the body.

Panpsychists who endorse this position tend to hold that mind and matter can only exist together. In other words, mind only exists "in" or "with" physical objects: a molecule may have some form of mindedness, but mind cannot exist separate from something physical. Mind cannot exist between bodies. Although, upon close inspection, the disagreements on this point can become confusing. Certainly, among some panpsychists, there are those who suggest that matter can have a "protomind" (see, for example, Benovsky, 2018). There are those who are clear that not all matter has a mind (a chair does not necessarily have the experience of what it's like to be a chair). But there are none who have claimed that mind can exist apart from matter. There is not a reference to mind with "protomatter," or assertions that not all instances of mind are embodied.

Yet the idea that mind can only occur together with matter may be challenged by the work of some other philosophers of mind. There are thinkers who have suggested that mind can "travel," so to speak. This is known as the extended mind hypothesis (Menary, 2010). The extended mind hypothesis is a philosophical argument in which it is demonstrated that the minds of humans are in part constituted by things (like a notebook or a computer) that exist in the environment (Clark & Chalmers, 1998). In the example that gave rise to the theory, Clark and Chalmers (2010) established that a person's cognitive processes—particularly memory and belief—can be created by the information stored in a notebook, which is external to the person whose mind it impacts. Since their seminal work, the view has been elaborated on by several other thinkers who have arrived at the conclusion that nearly all mental functions and states can be, in part, constituted by things that are outside of a person. How can mind be created between two things? If mind must be tied to matter, how can two separate physical entities co-create a mental experience? Shani and Keppler (2018) have suggested that perhaps sub-atomic particles, which are enminded, are exchanged between the mind of a person and an entity external to that person. There is another, perhaps simpler, way of conceiving of the extended mind, however. This is the position of many panpsychists known as cosmopsychism, to which we will turn momentarily.

1.3 Forms of Panpsychism

1.3.1 Bottom-Up Approaches

According to panpsychism, the phenomenon of what-it's-like is a fundamental aspect of reality. But this experience is not uniform; there are simpler and more complex forms of mind. Within panpsychism, there are very broadly two distinct approaches to questions regarding the relationship between simple forms of mind and complex consciousness, as is found in humans. The first approach is a "bottom-up" understanding that is analogous to the atomistic view of the physical world. A compound is composed of smaller units: elements. Elements are composed of molecules, which are composed of electrons, protons, and neutrons, which are composed of atoms, which are composed of even smaller units. It is the combination of very small units that creates the physical world. In the same way, many panpsychists believe that complex forms of consciousness are the result of combining small units of mindedness.

This bottom-up approach takes two different forms: constitutive panpsychism and emergent panpsychism. Constitutive panpsychism is basically the premise that microexperiences combine to create macroexperiences—very small versions of enmindedness, in which there is some experiential aspect but not necessarily consciousness (Bruntrup, 2017)—can combine to culminate in different, more advanced forms of consciousness, such as that exhibited by humans (Chalmers, 2017). Closely related is panprotopsychism. That is, fundamental physical entities have a form of protomindedness. From this perspective, there is nothing that it is like to be that entity, but there is the precursor of a mind associated with it. A full-blown experience, or macroexperience, is grounded in the protophenomenal properties of microphysical entities (Chalmers, 2017). That is, things like molecules or atoms (microphysical entities) have the precursor of a mind. When those microphysical entities come together, the protominds combine to create a mind.

An alternative to this view is emergent panpsychism. Emergent basically means that the whole is greater than the sum of its parts. From this perspective, a macroexperience (reflective consciousness) is strongly emergent from microexperiences (some basic experience of what it's like) (Chalmers, 2017). This means that something extra happens when small units are combined, something beyond just simple combination to create complex forms. These two positions—constitutive and emergent panpsychism—both suggest that, somehow, complex consciousness, such as that which we find in humans is the result of microexperiences or protominds coming together, just as molecules make elements and elements make compounds, etc. The cosmopsychist philosophers want to know what, precisely, is the process or mechanism by which small units can give rise to complex consciousness. The argument that is often used to support these approaches ends in some appeal to a fundamental law. As Philip Goff (2019a) pointed out, fundamental means that there is no further explanation. So, we are just left with the answer because that's the way it is. That answer is not good enough for some philosophers of mind.

1.3.2 Top-Down Approach: Cosmopsychism

The problem of how, exactly, small units of protomind or microexperience combine to give rise to complex consciousness is eliminated if one takes a different approach to the nature of fundamental consciousness. Cosmopsychism is a "top-down" approach to the nature of mindedness and complex consciousness. Instead of putting together small units to create larger entities, the cosmopsychist posits that the there is one primary entity: the universe. That is, it is based on the view that what is fundamental is not the smallest unit, but the largest entity:

> [E]xactly one *basic* concrete object, that is, the cosmos, exists . . . the cosmos is more basic than other concrete objects in the sense that it is ontologically prior to, or ontologically more fundamental than, those other objects.
>
> (Nagasawa & Wager, 2017, p. 115)

A good way to understand this is by looking at what we mean by fundamental. In the world of understanding matter, we say that smaller units are more fundamental than larger units. Let's look at water (H_2O). The larger unit, H_2O, cannot exist without hydrogen (H) and oxygen (O). But H and O could exist even if there was no such thing as H_2O. So, H and O are more fundamental than H_2O. Of course, they are not ultimately fundamental because the elements could not exist without electrons, atoms, etc. The point is that what is fundamental can exist in a world without more complex entities.

In cosmopsychism, the universe is the most fundamental thing. The earth, your liver, hydrogen, or atoms cannot exist apart from the universe. They cannot exist "outside" of the universe. This means that mind, or consciousness, is fundamental. Your consciousness cannot exist apart from or "outside of" the universal consciousness. Or, as Goff put it, "the universe is a conscious subject. All other things—from plants to human beings to fundamental particles—are conscious subjects that exist as proper parts of the universe subject" (Goff, 2019a, p. 108).

There is a single mind that is an aspect of the universe; and all of the smaller instances of mindedness are connected because they are part of the whole. We may be able to discern readily that the skin on my hand is connected to the skin on my foot. But it is also ultimately connected even to my lungs. Likewise, there is a single physical entity that is an aspect of the universe; and all of the smaller instances of matter are connected because they are part of the whole. Additionally, mind and matter are connected to each other by being aspects of the single whole. From this perspective, we can easily see that there are many instances where mind and matter exist simultaneously; that is, there are entities that have both a body and a mind. Sentient life-forms may be the most obvious example.

Goff (2019a) has argued that individual minds are grounded by subsumption in the universal mind. Subsumption means that an entity can be viewed as a complete unity that does not depend on the whole of which it is a part in order to grasp its essence. That is, the mind or consciousness of a particular person, or a cat, can be understood without necessarily having an understanding of cosmic consciousness, or of all the individual units within the fundamental singular mind. While an understanding of the universal mind is not necessary to understand the essence of a smaller unit, that unit is still a part of the singular mind; it has not spilt away from that in which it is grounded. Thus, a person's mind is a facet of the universal mind, even if it cannot directly experience the universal mind.

This raises the possibility that in contrast to the view that mind and matter must always co-exist in every instance, there may be instances in which each exists independently of the other within the cosmos. From a cosmopsychist perspective, it is only necessary for them both to be part of the universe, not to be together in every single manifestation within the universe. So, for example, a chair may not have a sense of what it's like to be a chair, or to be to sat upon, or to be broken. But there cannot be a universe in which there is a chair and there is no instance of mind at all. Likewise, there may be instances of a dis-embodied mind. If mind can exist independently of a physical structure, then it exists completely outside the constraints of time and space. This provides a much more elegant explanation of how the extended mind theory might work. No longer need one appeal to enminded sub-atomic particles being exchanged for minds to be connected or influence each other. Mind itself is simply exchanged or shared.

Kastrup (2017) expressed the relationship between the universal mind and the individual mind in a very interesting manner. He stated that the relationship is analogous to the process of dissociation as it is manifest in Dissociative Identity Disorder (DID). That is, he has suggested that individual minds are like alters in DID: "Dissociation can coherently explain how seemingly separate but concurrently conscious subjects of experience—such as you and me—can form . . . each is an alter of universal consciousness" (Kastrup, 2017, p. 17).

Shani (2015) has proposed seven basic postulates in relation to cosmopsychism. These postulates may prove to have value in an understanding of the nature of mind, particularly as it relates to issues important in psychotherapy.

The first postulate is that "the cosmos as a whole is the only ontological ultimate there is, and that it is conscious" (Shani, 2015, p. 408).

His second postulate is that:

> the cosmos as a whole is prior to its parts in the sense that every proper part of the cosmos depends on the whole, asymmetrically . . . the many exist in it, and through it, as 'moments', namely, as events of various durations, and as process configurations . . . no part, big or small, is either immutable or separable from the rest of nature.
>
> (Shani, 2015, p. 408)

The third postulate is "the lateral duality principle" (Shani, 2015, p. 410). That is, the universe, which is the ground of all being, is dual-natured. It has a revealed or explicit nature, which is the outer, observable expression of its concealed nature. The explicit nature is the regularity of the structural domain. The concealed or implicit nature of the universe is intrinsic and creative, and grounds the observable order of the universe.

The fourth principle is that the two aspects of the universe are differentially available to be known by observers. All observers exist within the universe. These observers experience the revealed nature of the universe as being physical—existing in space, having a structure, evolving in time, etc. This aspect of the universe is knowable through the scientific method. The concealed aspect of the universe is an intrinsically sentient medium, or a "vast ocean of consciousness" (Shani, 2005, p. 411). This aspect is not knowable through the same epistemological methods as the revealed/physical aspect of reality. What this means is that the scientific method is the best way to know about matter, but it cannot help us understand mind.

Shani's (2015) fifth postulate suggests a relationship between cosmic consciousness and individual consciousness; the former is a "deeper layer of consciousness grounding the particular streams of consciousness of individual creatures" (p. 412). Shani used the term "endo-phenomenal expanse" (2015, p. 413) to describe the universal ground, against which individual phenomenal states are the subjective experiences of "interference patterns" (2015, p. 413).

The sixth postulate Shani (2015) advanced is that individuals are "dynamic differentiations within the absolute" (Shani, 2015, p. 413), that are "interwoven in a continuous web of interrelationship, all are interconnected" (Shani, 2015, pp. 413–414). This interconnectedness can exist on several levels. So, for example, a whirlpool within an ocean can coalesce with other whirlpools to create a flow-pattern with a more complex structure, a mega-whirlpool if you will.

The seventh theoretical assumption Shani (2015) advanced in his formulation of cosmopsychism is that individuals, as local disturbances in the cosmic ocean, can become relatively stable systems. Like a whirlpool in the ocean, they maintain (for some period) a stable structure or pattern.

> This localization process consists . . . in the intensification and ordering of experience, as well as in the concentration of focus, within limited and relatively well-defined boundaries—creating a knot, or bulge of consciousness with an appearance of self-containment, which serves to separate the system's inner reality from the inner reality of the ocean surrounding it.
>
> (Shani, 2015, p. 418)

Shani and Keppler (2018) have further suggested that the nature of mind may mimic the actions of quantum particles in a field. Shani and Keppler pointed to the current acceptance among quantum physicists of the existence of the Zero Point Field (ZPF), which is the "origin of the quantum behavior of matter" (2018, p. 396). This activity (or process) is the "fields that mediate other fundamental forces" (Shani & Keppler, 2018, p. 396). System components typically demonstrate random (stochastic) motion. However, over time, the influence of the ZPF may induce the system to become coherent, and eventually phase-locked to maintain coherence or equilibrium with the ZPF. The philosophers describe the process this way:

> Due to the close interrelationship between material systems and the background field, the presence of matter also exerts influence on the internal structure and dynamics of the ZPF. This interplay induces a modification and partial organization of the local field in such a way that the relevant ZPF modes, which can be regarded as a system-specific set of resonance frequencies playing a dominant role in the maintenance of the balance situation, become *highly correlated* . . . . In other words, the orchestration of a dynamically stable system requires the initially chaotic ZPF to change over to a partially ordered state that shows a phase locking of the relevant field modes. As a result, . . . all the components of the system are effectively coupled through the ZPF, giving rise to collection cooperation and *long range coherence*.
>
> (Shani & Keppler, 2018, pp. 397–398, italics in original)

Cosmic consciousness is the ultimate mind field (or ZPF), with a network of mind fields within this whole. As we will see in Chapter 2, field theory is also important in psychoanalytic thought. The point here is that from pan-psychism, a theory of the nature of the mind (the thing we treat in psyh-chotherapy) begins to emerge. Based on the work of Shani (2015), we can hypothesize that each client's (and therapist's) mind is a relatively stable pattern within the vast ocean of the universal mind. As a stable pattern, it has a "set point" for experience—a typical way of perceiving and interpreting experiences. Yet, this set point is in fact dynamic. Thus, if the set point is contributing to the problems in living, it is amenable to change through psychotherapy. This set point gives one the feeling of individuality, or separateness or uniqueness, even when it combines with other individuals in a community (the mega-whirlpool). While this apparent isolation and uniqueness is highly important, all minds are ultimately connected through their being entities within a common or shared phenomenal field. This common substrate allows one mind to know, at least in part, another mind.

Shani and Keppler (2018) have detailed how this linking is mutative: in a field, linked elements pull each other into resonance, not only with each other but with the field itself. From this we may infer that psychotherapy is the process of helping a person change their mind through a purposeful connection with the therapist's mind.

This formulation of the nature of mind has within it a theory of how we can know the mind of another. We can know another's mind directly, without the mediation of words or other forms of paralinguistic communication. This is exactly what clinical intuition is.

1.4 Epistemology: Knowing Through Intuition

As noted previously, a meta-theory is comprised of an ontology and an epistemology. Ontology refers to the question of what is real, or the nature of reality. Our ontology here is cosmopsychism, which states that mind is real and fundamental, and, furthermore, the most fundamental unit of mind is the cosmos. Epistemology refers to views of how one comes to know reality. In this context, the question becomes how we can know mind. In particular, we want to help our clients come to know their own minds, and in order to be helpful in changing their minds we must know our clients' minds to some degree. Remember previously, Shani's (2015) explanation of the dual nature of the universe suggests that the physical universe is known through the scientific method. But measurement is not a way that we can know something that has no physical properties. Therefore, the way we can know mind must be by a different means.

The means by which we know mind is our ability to reflect on—or re-represent—qualia. The way we know the exogenous mind, that is, mind that is "outside" our little whirlpool of self-experience, is also through the registering of qualia. One quale that is important is the feeling of knowing. As we will see in the second part of this book, the feeling of knowing when you cannot identify the process by which you came to know something is intuition.

What this epistemology means in terms of therapy is that we help our clients to know their minds by helping them tune into qualia. We know, to some degree, our clients' minds by entering into a mental connection and sharing qualia. In order to accomplish these tasks, we hone our own intuition—both general intuition as well as the ability to apply intuition in a professional manner in the consulting room—and we teach our clients to access their own intuitions.

As we will explore, intuition is fallible. All epistemological tools are fallible. The preferred epistemological tool to help us understand the physical aspects of the universe is the scientific method. In this age of a replicability crisis, we are reminded that no one single experiment can give us infallible knowledge. It is not until we can confirm the results in repeated trials that we begin to have confidence in the knowledge we have gained. This situation is also the case with intuition. While we know that it is not infallible, there are ways to check the findings in order to gain greater confidence that we have acquired legitimate knowledge. Once again, these will be explored in detail in the second part of this book.

1.5 Practice Implications

I find the philosophy of mind to be fascinating. I hope you do too. But, I am a practitioner; and theory, to me, is meaningless unless we can apply it to our practice. What does cosmopsychism have to do with the way I do therapy? My objective is that the answers to this question will emerge throughout this book. But, right now, I'd like to reflect on cosmopsychism and therapy.

One implication is that we must appreciate the impact of living in a culture in which materialism is viewed as the only legitimate view of reality. In my experience, the world has been so overtaken by material monism that my clients come to me completely identified with their bodies. They come to me believing that they are the hapless victims of a disease of the brain. If medication can't help them, then they feel they must be stuck with a chronic, incurable disease. When I offer an exercise to a client to explore their minds, they tell me, "I can't do that. I have ADD." As I began to think about their problems in living from a cosmopsychist perspective, it occurred to me that my clients are "out of their minds." That is, they are so removed from their own minds that it has become very difficult to help them re-connect. But this re-connection is essential if they are to become whole again.

How do I help my clients re-connect to their minds? The first thing I do is introduce the idea that they have a mind that is not their body, and that changing their mind is the way out of their current problems in living. The process of seeing oneself as more than a body is quite impactful for many clients. Let me be clear: I help clients experience the integration of the mind and the body; I do not suggest that they ignore their bodies or that their minds are separate from their bodies. But I am clear and consistent with my clients these days that, in our work together, they can expect that our emphasis will be on their minds, which is not their brain or a neurological system.

An example of this process is my work with "Jody." Jody was convinced that her depression and anxiety were due to her being "neurodivergent." At one point she complained that "neurotypical people can't understand." This is a phrase that I hear a lot of clients echo. While the term technically suggests functioning on the autistic spectrum, it seems that in popular usage it is short-hand for suffering caused by a brain abnormality.

I explained to Jody that I don't believe that framing her difficulties as neurochemical will ultimately help her relieve her deep psychological suffering. "This is about changing your mind," I told her. "If this is about your brain, what you're telling me is that, unless I can alter your brain, you can't feel any better. That sounds pretty hopeless to me." I suggested that, as an experiment, we focus on her mind—on what it's like to feel sad and empty and lonely, and what it's like to feel self-conscious and like she doesn't fit in with others. "Let's see where we end up if we work as if this about helping you open up your mind to experience things differently, rather than on what your brain is capable or incapable of." Slowly, over time, as I repeated the injunction to "open your mind," Jody began to exercise greater effort toward appropriate self-regulation and to experience herself and her social interactions in new ways.

In Chapter 8, we will explore in greater detail the process of helping clients integrate the body and the mind. The point that I wish to make here is that when we do so, it is never with the idea that targeting neurochemical processes in the body will change the mind. Instead, it is always about reflecting on qualia—the experience of what-it's-like—that are associated with embodiment.

1.6 Conclusion

We have all been educated in a system that has taught us, sometimes explicitly and sometimes implicitly, that reality is composed of things that can be measured. Indeed, the father of psychotherapy himself developed his thoughts within this perspective. But contemporary philosophers of mind are calling this basic assumption into question. Their ideas have profound implications for what we psychotherapists do, and how we do it.

Let's take as a starting point the idea that mind is real, and that the mind of a client and the mind of a therapist are both facets of a single universal mind. They both feel separate and individual because that is the very nature of mind. They both tend to experience things according to repetitive patterns. And yet, the patterns are dynamic, that is, they can change. Part of the way they change is by coming into contact with other unique patterns, or other minds.

Minds, because they do not follow the laws of physics, can extend beyond bodies, and move between people. Some mental processes and contents can be shared. This is intuition. By using intuition in the clinical context, the therapist can know, in part, what it's like to be the client, or what it's like to be the client having a specific experience that is problematic.

The implication for therapy in the cosmopsychist paradigm is that the therapeutic work can be done to help clients change their minds through direct mental connectedness; talk therapy may involve communication that goes beyond talk and paralinguistic behaviors. The meta-theory has implications for how one views several issues that are key to psychotherapy, including what causes problems in living and how psychotherapy can help people resolve those problems. It will impact the goal of treatment as well as the interventions you use. It will influence your understanding of several core therapeutic concepts, such as the nature of consciousness and the sense of self. Thus, from this highly abstract discussion of philosophy, we will begin to understand what it means to practice MCDT.

1.7 Key Points

- Mind—the experience of what it's like—is real, even though you can't count it. It is not caused or created by neurochemical processes (the central nervous system or the brain). It is a fundamental aspect of the universe.

- The most basic form of mind is the universal mind, or cosmic consciousness. All other instances of mind (like yours, or your cat's) are a part of the universal mind.
- All of the parts (minds and bodies) of the universal whole are connected by virtue of their being parts of a single whole.
- Because mind is not matter, and therefore is not limited by the laws of nature or physics (space and time), mind can be extended beyond a single body.
- This means that two (or more) minds can connect. Two (or more) people can influence the minds of each other, and can share, to some degree (not entirely), mental experiences.
- This is intuition: two people sharing experience or qualia. Intuition becomes an important tool in how therapists can help their clients heal by changing their minds. It gives clients insight into their own minds, and how their minds are affected by others, as well as gives the therapist insight into what mental processes or contents may be contributing to the clients' problems in living.

1.8 References

Benovsky, J. (2018). *Mind and matter: Panpsychism, dual-aspect monism, and the combination problem.* Springer.

Bruntrup, G. (2017). Emergent panpsychism. In G. Bruntrup & L. Jaskolla (Eds.), *Panpsychism: Contemporary perspectives* (pp. 48–71). Oxford University Press.

Chalmers, D. J. (2017). Panspychism and panprotopsychism. In G. Bruntrup & L. Jaskolla (Eds.), *Panpsychism: Contemporary perspectives* (pp. 19–47). Oxford University Press.

Clark, A., & Chalmers, D. (1998). The extended mind. *Analysis, 58*(1), 7–19.

Clark, A., & Chalmers, D. (2010). The extended mind. In R. Menary (Ed.), *The extended mind* (pp. 28–42). MIT Press.

Goff, P. (2017). *Consciousness and fundamental reality.* Oxford University Press.

Goff, P. (2019a). *Galileo's error: Foundations for a new science of consciousness.* Pantheon Books.

Greenberg, J. R., & Mitchell, S. A. (1983). *Object relations in psychoanalytic theory.* Harvard University Press.

Harris, R. (2019). *ACT made simple* (2nd ed.). New Harbinger.

Kastrup, B. (2017). On the plausibility of idealism: Refuting criticisms. *Disputatio, 9*(44), 13–34.

Menary, R. (Ed.). (2010). *The extended mind.* MIT Press.

Mitchell, S. A. (1988). *Relational concepts in psychoanalysis: An integration.* Harvard University Press.

Nagasawa, Y., & Wager, K. (2017). Panpsychism and priority cosmopsychism. In G. Bruntrup & L. Jaskolla (Eds.), *Panpsychism: Contemporary perspectives* (pp. 113–129). Oxford University Press.

Shani, I. (2015). Cosmopsychism: A holistic approach to the metaphysics of experience. *Philosophical Papers, 44*, 389–437. https://doi.org/10.1080/05568641.2015.1106709

Shani, I., & Keppler, J. (2018). Beyond combination: How cosmic consciousness grounds ordinary experience. *Journal of the American Philosophical Association, 4*, 390–410. https://doi.org/10.1017/apa.2018.30

Depth Psychology Views of Mind

2

In the last chapter, we saw how philosophers of mind have defined the entity: mind is qualia, or the experience of what-it's-like. Examples of mind include such things as what it's like to bite into a ripe peach, what it's like to experience a trauma, or what it's like to be you. We saw in Chapter 1 that mind is one aspect of the universe and is just as real as matter. It cannot be explained as a side effect of our bodies or physiological processes. We also saw that mind does not occupy space. This means that is it not somewhere; it's not "in" me or you even though it is an aspect of me and you.

The mind that I experience exists as an instance of the universal mind. And although it's not "in" me, it feels like it is somehow a property of me or in some way "mine." Each of us experience qualia as happening to us—we have a sense of individuality and the feeling of a separate, bounded mind. This is an aspect of mindedness: all qualia are experienced as happening to me, even while they are an aspect of the universe, and as instances of, or grounded in, the universal mind.

MCDT is a combination of cosmopsychism and analytic thought. Therefore, in order to understand MCDT, it's important to understand how some analysts view mind. This chapter will focus on two key aspects of the analytic views of mind. The first is how the individual mind develops. Here, we will focus on Relational Theories of Development. The second is the distinction between the conscious mind and unconscious mind. Here the Jungian, and especially the post-Jungian, view of mind informs MCDT to a significant degree.

In understanding the analytic views of mind, we must remember that the analytic views came into being under the influence of materialism,

DOI: 10.4324/9781003090816-4

wherein mind was understood to be an epiphenomenon of the body. As we explored in Chapter 1, the materialist ontology, or view that physical processes are fundamental to mental processes, has played an important role in the development of theories of psychotherapy. Psychotherapy was born in a time when matter was believed to be the only fundamental aspect of reality. Foundational contributors to Relational Theory, Jay Greenberg and Stephen Mitchell (1983), noted that when Freud postulated mental structures, he expected to eventually confirm their anatomical location. Mitchell (1993) observed that many psychoanalytic thinkers continue to discuss mental processes as though they are material when they use physical-structural descriptions to discuss them. Today, there is burgeoning literature on mind-body unity. Yet, it appears that all of these accounts end in the notion that mind is a side effect of bodily processes, and the body is manipulated to change the mind.

While much of psychoanalytic thinking today is dominated by references to neuroscience and brain functioning, there are a few bastions that have maintained a focus on mind as simply mind. There are accounts of the purely mental features of problems in living with no attempt to explain these problems as being based on physical processes. In other words, they do not try to reduce all suffering to a pathology of the brain but remain focused on the subjective experience of the patient. These psychoanalytic thinkers emphasize the therapeutic value of clients having a greater awareness of and flexibility in their mental processes, states, and contents. They also stress the healing potential of the connection between the mind of the therapist and the client. MCDT is rooted in this latter approach.

2.1 Relational Theories of Development

Psychoanalytic theory is both a developmental theory and a treatment approach. Although there is not a singular view of normal human development among developmental analysts, there is agreement on many issues. Chief among these is the observation that the development of the human mind requires a connection with a more highly developed human mind.

The developmental literature that relates most closely to the development of the human mind is nestled in the research on the development of the sense of self. If one reads this literature closely, there are several observations that are relevant to an understanding of the development of mind. In reading the work for an eye toward this end, it is clear that Relational, Interpersonal, and Intersubjective Psychoanalytic Schools share the view that early in life the mind of the individual develops through connections with the minds of caregivers.

The idea that minds must be connected in order to grow and change has evolved a great deal since the early formulations by the Object Relations analyst John Bowlby, the father of attachment theory. The theories that dominated analytic thinking prior to Bowlby's work were centered on a view that infants are driven to maintain proximity to their mothers due to survival instincts (Bowlby, 1969/1982). Bowlby suggested that instead of being purely a question of secondary drive (that is, a drive that serves the survival drive), an infant's need to be with a caregiver (the mother in Bowlby's cultural/historical period) has "a biological function specific to itself" (Bowlby, 1969/1982, p. 179). That is, human infants, like other animals, need to be in relation to another of their species for reasons that transcend purely physical care (i.e., food and physical protection). He used the term "attachment" to signify this need, and particularly in reference to behaviors in which infants and caregivers engage in order to fulfill the need for proximity.

With the notion that attachment has greater significance than the physical survival needs of the infant, the developmental psychologist and analyst Daniel Stern (1985) researched how this relationship influences the development of the sense of self. Again, while his research was focused specifically on the sense of self, there are implications for the development of mind more broadly.

Stern's (1985) research suggests that from the moment of birth, the infant not only experiences the things that occur to and around them but they also experience the process of structuring these occurrences. This suggests that there is a mind, or experience of what it's like, from birth. This mind has not developed to include a sense of self, however. In order for this feat to be accomplished, the infant's mind must connect to a more mature, coherent, complex mind.

According to Stern (1985), attachment figures attune to their child in some circumstances. That is, the former adopts similar vocal and physical patterns as the child. Their voices match the rhythm and prosody as well as the rate and volume of the baby's cooing and babbling. Their bodies move in synchrony. Over time, the attuned caregiver and infant are able to achieve a state of shared inner experience (Beebe et al., 2005). In other words, their minds are, to some degree, working together and having very similar experiences. Stern (1985) discussed the process in physical terms: bodies attune, which *causes* the shared psychobiological state. But, as we shall see later, this process may be explained without recourse to physical causes. It may be more simply explained as an example of Menary's (2010) extended mind theory. In this case, instead of a mind being extended to include an inanimate object (like a notebook), a mind extends to encompass another mind.

Stern (1985) noted that caregivers have preferences and attune to their babies more readily when the baby is in certain states and do not attune to other states. This cues the baby on an implicit level that certain mental states are acceptable, and hence are safe to refine, expand, and experience again. Other subjective states and contents are not sharable, and hence are not elaborated on, refined, or re-experienced (Stolorow & Atwood, 1992). This creates a template that can operate long after infancy. The adult individual is able to comfortably recognize and use qualia that were shared and has great difficulty with qualia that were not shared. As we will explore more fully in the next chapter, this leads to later problems in living: those things for which clients seek psychotherapy. Stern (1985) gave the example of a baby whose mother attuned to her child readily when the latter evinced enthusiasm. This left the maturing child with the pattern of feeling that she must present as—indeed she must be—an enthusiastic, energetic person, even when it caused suffering for her to be so. A common experience therapists share is to have a client with whom the caregiver did not attune when the client showed anger in childhood. As adults, when anger is an important source of information, the client is not able to recognize, access, or use it appropriately. The point here is that when adult caregivers can share the mental state or contents of the infant, the infant can develop toward refining, expanding, and reflecting on those qualia. When the caregiver cannot share the mental state or contents, these qualia do not become part of, or are deleted from, the individual's conscious repertoire.

Tronick and his fellow members of the Process of Change Study Group (1998) also researched the adult regulation of an infant's physical and emotional states. His work and Stern's (1985) are highly consistent to the degree that, in both cases, findings suggest that an infant requires an external source—a caregiver—to develop mentally. Tronick and his colleagues' (1998) research demonstrated that the caregiver is required in order to maintain homeostasis. He illustrated his point with a biological example, but was clear that the same situation applies to emotional regulation:

> the maintenance of homeostasis is a dyadic collaborative process. Infants must collaborate with others to successfully regulate their physiological homeostatic states . . . the adult is part of the infant's homeostatic regulatory system: as much a part of any internal regulatory process.
>
> (Tronick et al., 1998, p. 293)

In keeping with the extended mind theory of philosophy (Menary, 2010), Tronick and his colleagues (1998) noted that an infant cannot regulate their core body temperature in isolation but is able to accomplish this task by connecting with an external source. While the infant may engage in behaviors to regulate core body temperature (for example, increasing movement to warm up), isolated attempts eventually fail. If the caregiver participates in the effort to warm up the baby (by holding them at their chest), the baby's core body temperature can maintain homeostasis. Tronick et al. explained this phenomenon in these terms: "These processes, internal and external, are functionally equivalent processes for regulating the infant's temperature. The internal and external mechanisms form a single system made up of two component systems (i.e., infant and mother)—a dyadic system" (Tronick et al., 1998, p. 293). To be sure, the group discussed the situation purely in terms of physical/material processes rather than as an extension of mind. As will be seen later, interpreting this work through a cosmopsychist lens allows us to postulate that the exchanges that drive this process may not be exclusively embodied forms of paralinguistic communication, and that regulation exceeds physical processes.

Tronick and his colleagues (1998) were clear: the dyadic connection that is established in experiences of mutual regulation "expand each individual's state of consciousness with powerful experiential and development consequences" (p. 295). The main point is this: there is a dyadic state of consciousness that is achieved during mutual regulation. This mental state has more components than that of either the mother or the infant alone. The dyadic state contains more information and is more complex and coherent than either possesses alone. Because the mother's state is more advanced than the infant's, the infant's mind benefits from an expansion of their potential mental processes, states, and contents to a greater extent than the mother's does.

Developmental research conducted by Stern (1985), Tronick et al. (1998), and other infant development researchers have all affirmed the notion that mind is shared from birth, and have emphasized the importance of the quality of shared mental experiences on psychological development. The attachment figure's ability to appropriately attune to the infant will influence the latter's mind in several areas. Among these are the sense of self (Stern, 1985; Fonagy et al., 2002); the ability to regulate affect, which Schore (2003) cites as the underlying factor in all psychopathology; and the ability to function socially (Fonagy et al., 2002). These central functions of mind exert a strong pull on how the individual will perceive and interpret experiences throughout their life course, or the possibility for what varied experiences can be like. The intersubjective experiences, or the shared mind between the attachment figure and the infant (and the experiences that are not shared), are thus understood to have long-term consequences for the mind and, thus, for the individual's quality of life.

The durability of these early experiences is explained by Stern's (1985) concept of representations of interactions that have been generalized (RIGs). Stern observed that an infant has the capacity to abstract from several related interactions and perceive an "average" from the aggregated specific incidents. The abstracted average experience then becomes represented preverbally. This representation continues to be updated as new specific incidents are fed into the RIG, although later incidents have less mutative value on the RIG than early experiences. The RIG is activated when a new situation occurs that has attributes in common with an existing RIG. This will affect the way that the person is able to experience the new incident. There is a tendency to experience something as just like—or at least as very similar to—the aggregated RIG. In this way, patterns of how one is able to perceive and interpret a new experience is reduced to a narrow range. As the RIG is preverbal, the fact that the new experience is filtered or distorted in this way remains outside of one's awareness. There is a sense, instead, that the here-and-now situation *is* the way that the subject experiences it: it is the only way the subject can experience it. This leads to both the distortion of experiences and a repetition of painful situations.

Thus, we see that the infant's mind develops optimally when another, more developed mind is able to share the mental state of the infant. Put another way, it is the connection between minds, and particularly the mental activity of a caregiver, that shapes the mind of the developing individual. Repeated experiences become templates for future experiences. It is the proclivity to repeat these patterns, even when doing so is problematic or inappropriate to the specific circumstance, that creates the problems in living that lead a client to seek psychotherapy, as we will see in the next chapter.

One further point regarding the shared mind is important here. The researchers cited previously have all stressed that the infant and the caregiver have a shared mental experience, and that it is the co-created nature of this experience that allows one to know the mental content or processes of another. Analyst and infant researcher Beatrice Beebe and her colleagues (2005) have added a significant piece: not only does the process of intersubjectivity, or the connection between minds, occur when two minds are having the same experience but difference is as important to intersubjectivity as sameness is; parents and therapists alike must be able to apprehend that the child or client is having a different experience. I am asserting here that this difference is just as knowable as similarity is through the process of connecting minds. In other words, we are able to apprehend another's qualia even when we are experiencing something dissimilar.

2.2 The Conscious Mind and the Unconscious Mind

In Chapter 1, we saw that panpsychist and cosmopsychist philosophers use the term "consciousness" to refer to complex states of mind. "The conscious" and "the unconscious" are extremely important constructs in psychoanalytic thought and practice. As MCDT is highly influenced by psychoanalytic thought, we might surmise that the terms are important to both the theory and practice of MCDT. Indeed they are, although the nomenclature is a bit different, based on the observations of a cosmopsychist philosopher.

2.3 A Cosmopsychist View of Consciousness and the Unconscious

For philosophers, the term "consciousness" is used to refer to complex states of mind. Mind, remember, means qualia, or the experience of what it's like. This leaves open the question of how, exactly, a complex mind differs from simple forms of mind. This question might be fruitfully answered by turning to the work of the philosopher of mind Bernardo Kastrup (2017).

Kastrup (2017) arrived at the conclusion that the difference between the two forms of mentation ("conscious" and "unconscious") is the ability to introspectively identify (or re-represent) qualia and report on them. That is, what the analysts call conscious experiences are those that we are able to reflect on and symbolically represent. A common form of symbolic representation among humans is language. This means that complex states of mind are qualia that one can reflect on and talk about. His suggestion is that what we normally refer to as a conscious thought is actually an instance of meta-consciousness (Kastrup, 2017).

Kastrup (2017) stressed that it is not necessary to reflect on an experience or verbalize it in order to experience something. You can have experiences that you do not identify, reflect on, and report. Kastrup (2017) was clear that he did not prefer to term these experiences as "unconscious," as they are instances of mind or consciousness. There can be no experience that is not some form of consciousness. Thus, for Kastrup (2017), there is meta-consciousness and consciousness, rather than consciousness and the unconscious.

2.4 Analytic Views of Consciousness and the Unconscious

The term "depth psychology" refers to therapies that work with the unconscious. Perhaps the two most notable forms of therapy that include explorations of the unconscious are psychoanalysis and analytical psychology. The psychoanalytic schools are those theories and practice approaches whose adherents claim descent from Freud. Analytical psychology includes analysts and therapists who claim descent from Jung. Just as the Relational, Intersubjective, and Interpersonal Analysts have continued to develop Freud's theories, and depart from them in important ways, post-Jungians have made important changes to Jung's understanding of the unconscious. These changes, blended with a cosmopsychist view of mind and consciousness to form the view of mind that is central to MCDT.

Typically, in analytic circles, the term "conscious" refers to mental processes and contents that we are aware of. In Freud's topographic model, mind is viewed as an iceberg. The portion of the iceberg that is above the water, and readily visible, is the conscious mind: that of which we are aware. Just below the surface is the preconscious: things that we are not currently aware of but which we can bring into awareness easily. Finally, there is the bulk of the iceberg/mind: the unconscious. This is the vast expanse of mental processes and contents that are outside of our awareness. In spite of the fact that we are not aware of these processes or the contents of this part of our minds, they nonetheless play an important role in our mental lives. They affect how we perceive and interpret all that we experience and, thus, shape our very awareness, even while they remain outside of it.

According to Freud, there are experiences we don't want to have or to have had. In the language of MDCT, there are qualia that we reject. Freud determined that we refuse these experiences by employing any one of a number of defensive operations; perhaps among the best known of the defenses are repression, suppression, or denial. The list is much longer. These qualia don't go away, however. They move out of our awareness, or out of our capacity to reflect on them; they become unconscious.

Even though we are not aware of them, unconscious contents continue to exert an influence on us. The unconscious leaks into our lives by causing behaviors and symptoms that are problematic. So, for example, I may be sharp with my partner when he asks me a reasonable question. I do so because I am not aware of the fact that I am frustrated with a task related to work. My frustration from work, which I do not want to experience, thus leaks out onto my interaction with my partner. There are likewise mental processes that we are not aware of. Employing the defenses may be the most obvious of the mental processes that we keep out of our awareness.

For Freud, in order to get rid of the symptom, you have to identify, through inference, the underlying problematic unconscious contents from the ways that they leak out. He used free association to weaken the boundary between the conscious and the unconscious in order to find the unconscious experiences at the root of the problem.

2.4.1 Relational Analysts and the Unconscious

Fast forward almost 100 years. Many analysts have found that those processes and contents that are unconscious are often so because of interactions with other important people, such as caregivers early in life. They also found that understanding unconscious processes and contents as falling into different categories can be helpful. The Intersubjective Analysts, Stolorow and Atwood (1992), identified three realms of the unconscious. First, there is the prereflective unconscious. This refers to those organizing principles that operate outside of awareness. The organizing principles can aid in the process of becoming aware of something and they can block awareness, such as the process of employing defenses. The prereflective unconscious is non-defensive; we are unaware of these processes, not because we actively push them away but because we have simply never been able to reflect on them.

The second realm, the dynamic unconscious, is defensive. These are the contents that are pushed out of consciousness because they have threatened needed ties to other people. Important people in our lives reacted in a negative manner, tacitly or actively threatening abandonment or abuse in response to registering that we have experienced something forbidden. So, for example, if a caregiver harshly chastises a child for expressing anger, that child may push anger out of their awareness when it arises in the future. This does not mean that they are not affected by anger. They are not only affected by their anger but also are likely to act on it. But they cannot discern that they are angry. According to the Intersubjective Theory, the dynamic unconscious can be made conscious only with great effort.

The third form the unconscious takes in Intersubjective Theory is the unvalidated unconscious. This is the material that never evoked validating responsiveness from other people. Here there is no defensive exclusion of material that threatened to break into one's awareness. Instead, there is a hole. The caregivers did not respond negatively, but rather they did not respond at all.

For example, a child may lie in bed at night and hear their parents make terrible sounds of banging, yelling, and screaming. If the next morning nobody says anything about the incident and the parents act as if nothing untoward happened, the experiences of the night will be consigned to the child's unvalidated unconscious. The subjective experience was not able to become fully formed in an interpersonal context. They will not be available for reflection, elaboration, or representation. Of importance here is the idea that we cannot become aware of an experience unless we share it (or have previously shared something like it) without another mind. It takes two minds to create and maintain consciousness, or awareness of mental contents.

The Interpersonal Analysts also recognized that the unconscious is not a singular phenomenon. Stern (1995) recognized two forms of the unconscious: the dynamic unconscious and the cognitive unconscious. The former is comprised of contents: impulses that do not fit with the sense of self. You may see yourself as a peaceful, understanding, reasonable person; you may not become aware of the fact that you experienced an impulse to punch the person who just insulted your child. As a result, these contents get split off from the conscious personality. The impulses press for conscious representation. According to Stern (1995), the contents of the dynamic unconscious can take one of two paths: either they have been reflected on, then repressed, or they were never reflected on at all. In the former case, a person is at least dimly aware of them but then drives them out of awareness. Stern (1995) used the term "unformulated experience" to refer to experiences that have never been reflected on at all.

The cognitive unconscious is made up of the mental processes (perception, attention, memory, etc.) or "templates and screens" (Stern, 1995, p. 120) through which we identify which stimuli will be elaborated on as meaningful. These processes do not press for conscious representation. They are associated with the social processes that exert restraint on what can and cannot be experienced. This restraint operates through language; through language, society determines which thoughts, feelings, and experiences are stigmatized and, therefore, repressed. Like the Intersubjective Theory, the Interpersonal Analysts recognize the social requirement for material to become conscious. That is, they must be shared to enter awareness.

Sullivan (1953/1997) used the term "selective inattention" (failure to notice) to identify at least part of what is meant by the unconscious. It is a normal process that gates stimulation. We have to unconsciously recognize and screen out stimuli, or else we would be overwhelmed. While the process usually operates naturally and is not involved with pathology, we can use this process defensively to blinker that which we do not want to recognize.

Through selective inattention, we perpetuate the patterned ways of perceiving and interpreting experiences. This point is crucial to MCDT and will be elaborated on in the next chapter. What is important here is that one of the reasons a person fails to notice something is that the experience was not responded to by the caregiving surrounding them, like the unvalidated unconscious in the Intersubjective School.

The Interpersonal and Intersubjective Analysts agree that in order for us to be able to become aware of something, it must have been responded to by caregivers. This means that consciousness (awareness) is an interpersonal, intersubjective experience. It is the result of two (or more) minds recognizing an experience, and to some degree sharing it.

We must also understand the role of culture and the shared language in a culture in determining what we can become aware of. If a culture and that culture's language defines an experience in a specific way, it is difficult to deviate from that experience (but not impossible). For example, if a culture places people in binary categories, like black and white, it is difficult to experience someone as bi-racial. We see that in American history: bi-racial people were experienced by the majority culture as black for a very long time. We see this in the binary notion of gender, as well. The examples could be multiplied. The point is, if a culture does not recognize an experience, it is very difficult for an individual within that culture to have the experience on a conscious level.

In summarizing the analytic view of the conscious, we see that the key word is "awareness." Much as Bernard Kastrup (2017) suggested in relation to meta-consciousness, a conscious experience is one in which there is the ability to reflect on the experience and represent it symbolically, or talk about it. For an experience to be unconscious, it is necessary that we were either never aware of it or it bubbles up to awareness and we defensively push it out of our field of representation. From the Relational Perspective, what we can be aware of is highly influenced by caregivers and the culture in which we are embedded. In other words, conscious experience is qualia that was shared by two or more minds.

2.5 Jungian Unconscious

Perhaps one of the biggest enduring differences between the Relational Analysts and the work of Jung is the difference in the view of the unconscious, and hence the meaning of consciousness. Jung saw the unconscious as having two domains. He identified the personal unconscious as being comprised of "lost memories, painful ideas that are repressed (i.e., forgotten on purpose), subliminal perceptions, which are meant sense-perceptions that were not strong enough to reach consciousness and finally, contents that are not yet ripe for consciousness" (Jung, 1953/1972, para. 103). This definition has a great deal of overlap with the Relational Analysts view of the unconscious. Although, the necessity for minds to share an experience in order for it to become conscious appears to be absent.

The second domain of the unconscious for Jung is the collective unconscious. Jung identified the personal unconscious as being a "superficial level" of the unconscious. He used the terms "impersonal unconscious" and "transpersonal unconscious" as well as "collective unconscious" to refer to a deeper level of unconsciousness. He described it as "detached from anything personal and is common to all men" (Jung, 1953/1972, para 103). He described the collective unconscious as being "primordial images" and "inherited thought-patterns" that are inborn and universal; it is the "common psychic substrate" (Jung, 1959/1990, para. 3) of all humankind, throughout history and across cultures, expressed in literature, myths, and fairytales.

Thus, for Jung, the collective unconscious is the mental content that is shared by all humans. Just as all humans share a heartbeat, they share certain mental experiences that are tied to the human condition. For example, most people the world over at the time he wrote had, and indeed were raised by, a biological mother and a biological father. Thus, the meaning of mother and father assume archetypal importance that Jung held to be a common human experience. It is important to note that Jung stated that the collective unconscious, and the archetypes that reside therein, are psychological, not metaphysical, phenomena (Jung, 1953/1972, para. 151). But the question of where they are located has been subject to disagreement among Jungians.

The Jungian analyst Jeffrey Raff (2000) has taken a close look at this question and arrived at a conclusion that he sees as differentiating himself from Jung's original intent. For Raff, there is a difference between the psyche and the psychoid (similar to, but different from, the psyche). He describes that for Jung, archetypes emanate from the psyche. Raff emphasized that they "are clearly imaginal and derived from the psyche. These figures feel as if they were coming from within oneself" (Raff, 2000, p. 29). He reiterates that they "originate in the inner, unconscious world" (Raff, 2000, p. 31). He juxtaposes this experience of inner figures with psychoid figures, which feel external to the self. They are "beings that exist independently of the imaginative facility" (Raff, 2000, p. 30). Because psychoid figures possess a subtle body, they are capable of having an effect on the external world, as in the kinds of transformations that occur to substances during the alchemical process. Thus, we see that for at least some Jungians, there are beings that manifest in the minds of those who invite them.

It is particularly interesting in the context of this book that Raff's ontology is parallel to the cosmopsychist worldview. He quotes his teacher and analyst Marie von Franz, an early student of Jung's: "there exists in nature and in the collective unconscious, at least potentially, a kind of objective consciousness or mind from which the individual ego-consciousness is derived only secondarily and through which it is expanded by 'illumination'" (von Franz, 1996, p. 171, cited in Raff, 2000, p. 44). Thus, we see that Jungian theory of the unconscious includes those who understand the collective unconscious to be associated with a universal mind that is the ground of being for individual minds.

Jung developed a method that was different from his teacher's in order to make known the material that resided in the unconscious. In order to understand his method of active imagination, it may be helpful to first look at his theory of the two modes of thought, an idea that he borrowed from the work of William James. One mode of thought is linear, discursive, and symbolically represented in language. This is a problem-solving mode that is related to objective reality. The second form of thinking is more fantasy-oriented. It is carried out by means of images and feelings. It is this form of thinking that gives one entrée into the unconscious, both personal and collective.

Jung used this second form of thinking to help clients gain awareness of unconscious material. By using the imagination, one creates an image. This image can be anthropomorphic, theriomorphic, or any other physical depiction. After calling forth this image, the person engages with it in some manner. This can be through dialogue, through tracking associations, or through noting reactions (Chodorow, 1997). In this way, the contents of the unconscious become known.

2.5.1 Post-Jungians and Transpersonal Psychology

Just as the Freudian lineage has evolved, Jungian analytical psychology has continued to change. Today, there are a number of thinkers who are sometimes identified as "post-Jungian." They are highly indebted to Jungian thought and have equally departed from it. An early post-Jungian, James Hillman (1975), appears to buck the notion of a monistic world-view. In his book *Re-Visioning Psychology*, he calls for a move away from what he calls a monotheistic psychology and consciousness in favor of a polytheistic psychology and consciousness. On the level of psychology, he rejects the notion that a person is the locus of a single psyche. Rather, humans exist within the psyche. This may be interpreted as very near the cosmopsychist worldview.

Richard Tarnas is a post-Jungian scholar and was influenced by Hillman's work. He expanded on the Jungian concept of archetypes. In doing so, he asserted that the nature of consciousness is participatory. That is, there is a single, universal consciousness that exists in a reciprocal, mutually co-created relationship with the consciousness of individuals. He discussed the participatory nature of consciousness in the context of epistemology, or how it is that we can know about reality. But, his work is premised on an implicit ontology, or a view of the nature of reality. He is clearly in line with the cosmopsychist philosophers in that he views consciousness as a singular, pervasive phenomenon. According to Tarnas, the universe is "a fundamentally and irreducibly interconnected whole, informed by creative intelligence and pervaded by patterns of meaning and order that extend through every level" (2006, p. 77). He further elaborated on his ontology as "a universe in which mind and matter, psyche and cosmos, are more pervasively related or radically united than has been assumed in the modern world view" (Tarnas, 2006, p. 77). This emphasis on two phenomena of equal status—mind and matter—as twin aspects of a unitary whole brings him to the doorstep of cosmopsychism.

This understanding is premised on the awareness the "human being is a microcosm within the macrocosm of the world, participating in its interior reality and united with the whole in ways that are both tangible and invisible" (Tarnas, 2006, pp. 16–17). Against either the assertion of Logical Positivism, that the world is devoid of subjectivity, or of Constructivism, that the world is a projection of human subjectivity, is the participatory position that the world is itself subjective, or has a "capacity for intentional significance" (Tarnas, 2006, p. 21). Human subjectivity in this model exists in a relationship of mutual and reciprocal co-creation with the world.

Thus, the post-Jungians have brought us full circle. They have suggested that there is a single, unified universe. This universe is conscious. However, in distinction from the cosmopsychists, the post-Jungians posit that the relationship between the consciousness of the universe and that of an individual is not a one-way relationship: the universal conscious is not the ground of individual consciousness, but instead both create and are created by all separate instances of consciousness. This may be, again, an interesting metaphysical speculation. But it must be more than that to be useful. As we will see as the book unfolds, this relationship between universal consciousness and the individual mind is the mechanism for change in MCDT.

2.6 Rapprochment

Robin S. Brown is an analyst who has called for a reunion between the Freudian and Jungian branches of depth psychology. His ultimate aim has been to admit metaphysics and spirituality into clinical work. To this end, he has suggested that we view our work through a panpsychist lens. On the basis of this agenda, he has coined the term "post-relational" for his approach to clinical work.

In *Psychoanalysis Beyond the End of Metaphysics* (2017), Brown eschewed the bio-reductionist view that consciousness is caused by neurological functions. In *Groundwork for a Transpersonal Psychoanalysis* (2020), he delves into the philosophical underpinnings of the notion of the unconscious. In so doing, he supports a view of the unconscious that is not only not biological but also is multifaceted and represents a continuum of the intensity of mentation. In other words, there is not a dichotomy between the conscious and the unconscious, but a range in one's capacity to reflect on an experience. Perhaps more importantly, Brown wove together a philosophical argument for an understanding of an unconscious ground as the "original unity out of which self and other emerge" (2020, p. 7); it is a "unificatory principle" (2020, p. 8) that ties together the mind and the body, the self and the world. An appreciation of this unity may be a bridge that can connect Relational and post-Jungian Psychologies. In blending these approaches, Brown arrives at a "radically communal approach to the psyche" (Brown, 2020, p. 26).

The work of cosmopsychist philosopher Bernard Kastrup has led to the conclusion that the difference between conscious experience and unconscious experience is the degree to which one is able to reflect on and symbolically represent an experience. Relational Analysts have argued that in order for an experience to be conscious—that is, in order for a person to be able to reflect on that experience and put it into words—it must have been recognized and shared by another person. That is, two or more minds must have shared the experience.

From the post-Jungians, we borrow the view that complex mind or consciousness exists beyond the individual. And rather than it being the ground or source of human experience, the individual mind and the transpersonal (beyond the individual) mind are in a complex process of mutual, reciprocal co-creation. These orienting views taken from cosmopsychism, Relational Analysis, and post-Jungians bring us to the view of consciousness and the unconscious in Mind-Centered Dynamic Psychotherapy.

2.7 Practice Implications

As I have used my developing perspective to work with clients, I have found it generally easier to do away with the notion that I am working on a conscious or unconscious level, or that the client and I are processing conscious or unconscious material or processes. I have come to understand consciousness more in keeping with the cosmopsychist ontology: consciousness is an aspect of the universe in which humans participate. Rather than use the terms "conscious" and "unconscious" in the therapeutic context, I think in terms of one's ability to reflect on experiences and processes or not. In keeping with Brown (2020), I see the matter as a continuum. At one end, there are experiences that one cannot imagine. I view them rather as the absence of experience. It does not even occur to you to try to imagine such a thing. Yet, you may experience something tomorrow that you never dreamt could be—it exists in the universe and, thus, as a potential experience for a given sentient being. Up the continuum there are experiences proper. Among these, there are those that you can reflect on and those that you do not reflect on. Concerning the latter, there are two kinds of experiences: those that you have not (yet) represented and put into words and those that you have rejected, that you work to keep from reflecting on. Further up the continuum are those experiences that you are able to represent symbolically and reflect on, those which have been shared with another mind. I term these different relationships to experience as "the unimagined" for the first kind of qualia; "the unformulated" (after Stern, 1995) for experiences that we have had but never reflected on; "the unwelcome" for those experiences we reject; and "the represented" for experiences that are typically termed "conscious" by the analysts.

How we work with clients with a particular problematic pattern of experiencing depends on where on the continuum they are in relation to the way they are experiencing the phenomenon now, and where they are in relation to the potential to experience it. There are four possibilities: the client may have a wholly new experience that they have never even imagined previously, they may represent an experience that was previously not represented, they may accept an experience that they have rejected, or they may make changes in the way that they represent experiences that they have reflected on.

2.8 Conclusion

In the first chapter, I developed a cosmopsychist view of mind that suggests that what feels like "my" mind is actually a dynamic pattern within the sea of mind. In this chapter, we saw that these individual instances of mind can combine with other such individual minds, and that in so doing each achieves an expanded state.

After reviewing a brief history of depth psychology, I stressed repeatedly that this connection of minds is at the very center of Relational Analytic Thought regarding how minds grow and develop. Implicit here is the notion that healing is growth or development in a specific direction. One of the ways that the joining of minds contributes to development is that a person can reflect on and verbalize (or become conscious of) only those experiences that have been shared with another through such a mental connection. Other experiences are "conscious" in the panpsychist sense, in that they exist within the universal consciousness. This is where Jungian psychology—and particularly some post-Jungian formulations—can enhance the relational view: by understanding "the unconscious" as going beyond individual experience. Because the terms used differently in these ways can cause some confusion, I have found it easier to think of an experience or mind as existing on a continuum: from the unimagined, to the unformulated, to the unwelcome, up to the reflected forms of qualia. As we will see in the next chapter, opening one's mind to be able to experience the unimagined and the unformulated, as well as changing one's relationship to both the unwelcome and the reflected forms of qualia, is at the center of the healing process.

2.9 Key Points

- Individual minds must connect in order for growth and healing to occur.
- An individual mind can only be aware of, reflect on, and verbalize or re-represent (i.e., be conscious of) experiences that have been shared with another mind.
- Experiences that are "unconscious" exist as part of the universal consciousness, even if a person cannot reflect on them. Thus, they are potentially available to everyone.
- Experiences that are not reflected upon and/or are driven from awareness (i.e., unconscious), nonetheless, influence an individual.
- Psychotherapy, thus, requires that the therapist and client join minds as part of the growth/healing process.

2.10 References

Beebe, B., Knoblauch, S., Rustin, J., & Sorter, D. (2005). *Forms of intersubjectivity in infant research and adult treatment*. Other Press.

Bowlby, J. (1969 / 1982). *Attachment* (2nd ed.). Basic Books.

Brown, R. S. (2020). *Groundwork for a transpersonal psychoanalysis.* Routledge.

Brown, R. S. (2017). *Psychoanalysis beyond the end of metaphysics.* Routledge.

Chodorow, J. (Ed.). (1997). *Jung on active imagination.* Princeton University Press.

Fonagy, P., Gergely, G., Jurist, E. L., & Target, M. (2002). *Affect regulation, mentalization, and the development of the self.* Other Press.

Greenberg, J. R., & Mitchell, S. A. (1983). *Object relations in psychoanalytic theory.* Harvard University Press.

Hillman, J. (1975). *Re-visioning psychology.* Harper.

Jung, C. G. (1953 / 1972). On the psychology of the unconscious (R. F. C. Hull, Trans.). In H. Read et al. (Series Eds.), *The collected works of C. G. Jung* (Vol. 7, pp. 13–119). Princeton University Press. (Original work published in 1917).

Jung, C. G. (1959 / 1990). The archetypes and the collective unconscious (R. F. C. Hull, Trans.). In H. Read et al. (Series Eds.), *The collected works of C. G. Jung* (Vol. 9, part 1, pp. 3–72). Princeton University Press. (Original work published in 1934).

Kastrup, B. (2017). There is an "unconscious", but it may be conscious. *Europe's Journal of Psychology, 13*(3), 559–572. https://doi.org/10.5964lejop.v13.1388

Menary, R. (Ed.). (2010). *The extended mind.* MIT Press.

Mitchell, S. A. (1993). *Hope and dread in psychoanalysis.* Basic Books.

Raff, J. (2000). *Jung and the alchemical imagination.* Nicolas Hays.

Schore, A. N. (2003). *Affect dysregulation and disorders of the self.* W. W. Norton & Co.

Stern, D. B. (1995). Cognition and language. In M. Lionells, J. Fiscalini, C. H. Mann, & D. B. Stern (Eds.), *Handbook of interpersonal psychoanalysis* (pp. 79–138). Routledge.

Stern, D. N. (1985). *The interpersonal world of the infant: A view from psychoanalysis and developmental psychology.* Basic Books.

Stolorow, R. D., & Atwood, G. E. (1992). *Contexts of being: The intersubjective foundations of psychological life.* The Analytic Press.

Sullivan, H. S. (1953 / 1997). In Classic and groundbreaking synthesis of psychoanalysis, psychology and social science. H. S. Perry & M. L. Gawel (Eds.), *The interpersonal theory of psychiatry.* W. W. Norton & Co. (Originally published in 1953 by the William Alanson White Psychiatric Foundation).

Tarnas, R. (2006). *Cosmos and psyche: Intimations of a new world view.* Plume.

Tronick, E. Z., Bruschweiler-Stern, N., Harrison, A. N., Lyons-Ruth, K., Morgan, A. C., Nahum, J. P., Sander, L., & Stern, D. (1998). Dyadically expanded states of consciousness and the process of therapeutic change. *Infant Mental Health Journal, 19*(3), 290–299.

von Franz, M. (1996). *Aurora consurgens.* Pantheon.

How Problems Arise, and How Psychotherapy Helps to Heal Them

3

By synthesizing cosmopsychism with Relational and post-Jungian views of mind, we arrive at an understanding of what mind is and how it develops. Mind is qualia, or the subjective sense of what-it's-like. Furthermore, we all experience qualia as happening to me; thus, there is a sense of individuality that is an aspect of mind. The individually experienced mind is a dynamic pattern within the sea of the universal mind. There is a reciprocal co-creation between the "individual" mind and the universal mind, as well as between individual instances of mind. Thus, individual minds can influence each other when coupled. When experiences are shared with another mind, the individual is able to reflect on them, or re-represent them and put them into words. When another mind cannot or will not or has not shared our experience, those phenomena are not available for reflection. They nonetheless exert an influence on our functioning. Now we will turn to an account of how this developmental process is implicated in the kinds of problems in living that clients bring to therapy. We will also explore how MCDT works to help clients find relief from their suffering.

In psychotherapy, how do we make the moment-to-moment decisions about what to say or not say? Clients share very complex feelings, meanings, and narratives. Which thread do we follow, while leaving several other threads unplucked? What you do, what you explore, and the way you respond depends on what you see as the underlying causes of problems in living, and how you understand therapy to trigger change. How you conceive the underlying reasons people are experiencing difficulties, and what you understand the mechanisms of change to be, will guide the intervention. If you think that

DOI: 10.4324/9781003090816-5

mind is a by-product of neurochemical processes, then problems in living are due to a "disease of the brain," and the best way to change a mind is to alter a client's neurochemistry. The most direct way to do this is with medication or direct manipulation of the body. If you think that mind is real and fundamental, and grows and changes in connection with other minds, then knowing how to use your mind to help your client change their mind is going to be a top priority.

Much of infant development research and psychoanalytic thinking today is dominated by references to neuroscience and brain functioning. For those researchers and theorists who explain the development of the mind in terms of neurochemical processes, MCDT uses a cosmopsychist meta-theory to re-interpret their findings to arrive at a theory of the development of mind that is purely mental. This is a difference between some Relational Psychoanalytic Theories and MCDT.

Having clarified this important difference between some of the theories reviewed here and MCDT, the theories that are central to analytic thought are also at the heart of MCDT. The researchers and analytic thinkers reviewed here emphasize the therapeutic value of clients having a greater awareness of and flexibility in their mental processes, states, and contents. They also stress the healing potential of connection between the mind of the therapist and the client.

3.1 How Problems Arise From the Relational Perspective

As we explored in Chapter 2, the developmental analysts stress that the human mind is shaped in connection with other minds. Like the extended mind theory discussed in Chapter 1, the developmental research suggests that a mind is not encapsulated within a body. Instead, individual minds exist beyond the body and can exert an influence on each other.

Another point that is stressed by the developmentalists is that the way that one's mind is shaped in these early interactions can provide a pull throughout the life course. That is, early experiences form generalized representations, which in turn influence the way that future events will be experienced. Early experiences become the filter through which later experiences are perceived and interpreted. Mind, or the way that we tend to experience things, structures future encounters. In this way, highly patterned ways of experiencing are continually reinforced. The analytic therapists stress that, under certain circumstances, those patterns are applied with a high degree of rigidity. This impairs a person's ability to have novel experiences. This, the Relational Analysts suggest, is the cause of problems in living. The rigidity of representations is associated with emotional pain.

This understanding of what causes problems in living gives rise to the common goals of treatment proposed by Relational, Interpersonal, and Intersubjective Schools of Analysis. Mitchell (1993) posited that the goal of Relational Psychoanalysis to help the client break free of constraining templates to be able to have new, vitalizing experiences. The goal of Interpersonal Psychoanalysis is highly consistent with Relational Theory: it is to break the loop in which the patient generates "the same perceptions of self and others over and over again" (Cooper, 1995/2015, p. 691). Likewise, the goal of Intersubjective Psychoanalysis is consistent with the Relational and Interpersonal Schools. It is to help the patient change the way that they structure experience so that they can:

> achieve an optimal balance between the maintenance of his psychological organization, on the one hand, and his openness to new forms of experience, on the other. On the one hand, his psychological structures have become sufficiently consolidated so that they can assimilate a wide range of experiences of self and other and still retain their integrity and stability. His subjective world, in other words, is not unduly vulnerable to disintegration or dissolution. On the other hand, his psychological structures are sufficiently flexible to accommodate new configurations of experience of self and other so that the organization of his subjective life can continue to expand in both complexity and scope.
>
> (Stolorow & Atwood, 1994, p. 27)

The more inclusive group of Relational Analysts agree that rigid patterns of experience are projected onto new situations, and keep the individual locked in re-experiencing painful qualia. Some analysts have suggested an additional developmental pathway for pathology. Fonagy and his associates (2002) have suggested that mental development is derailed when the caregiver is unable to hold the infant's mind in their mind. These researchers have demonstrated that infants are born with a capacity to detect contingency. That is, they are aware when a caregiver's vocal and facial displays are consistent with the infant's internal experience. In order for the infant's sense of self to develop normally, they must experience this contingency, or, as Fonagy and his team of researchers have stated, they must see their mind in the caregiver's mind. When parental caregiving is insensitive and mis-attuned, this does not happen. The infant experiences just the caregiver's mind instead. The infant internalizes the representation of the caregiver's state of mind as part of their own. Their ability to reflect on their own subjective experience, and the ability to differentiate between those experiences that are genuinely "theirs" (endogenous, as will be explored later) and those that are emanating from their caregiver's (or exogenous) mind is impaired.

In my clinical experience, I have repeatedly worked with clients who present with feeling states that are very uncomfortable and that they are unable to regulate. Upon close inspection, we find that these clients are highly susceptible to contaiging other people's affect, and identify it as their own. They have remained unsuccessful in learning how to regulate the state in part due to the fact that they are misattributing the source. This will be explored in detail in the next chapter. The point that is important here is this: besides rigidity being pathogenic, misattributing the source of qualia can cause mental suffering.

These observations suggest that the cause of clients' problems is the way that their minds were shaped or limited in early interactions with their caregivers. When the caregiver could not share an experience, the growing child could not reflect on that experience. In the psychoanalytic nomenclature, the experience is consigned to the unconscious, or personal unconscious in Jungian terms. The ability to reflect on and symbolically represent (i.e., talk about) an experience allows one to develop and elaborate on experiences, building flexibility. When they cannot reflect on the experience, it becomes locked in a rigid application across contexts, or continually projected. The person is left with a too-narrow range in ways they can experience. The goal of therapy is to bring greater flexibility to the way that a person is able to experience, or to have new and different experiences.

We see echoes of this perspective in Jungian thought. According to Hall and Nordby (1973), in Analytical Psychology, the ego is the process that provides organization in the conscious mind. It is a sort of filter that prohibits anxiety-provoking experiences from becoming conscious. According to Jungian theory, the healthier a person is, the less likely it is that an experience will provoke anxiety and, thus, the ego will allow more varied types of experiences to become conscious. Consistent with the Relational Analytic Schools, limitations in the ability to have new experiences are associated with problems in living.

Add to this the Jungian concept of complexes. These are relatively autonomous aspects of the personality that operate outside of one's awareness. Vesey-McGrew (2010) has stressed that they are rigid patterns in how we experience the self and the other. Drawing on the work of John Perry (1970), she suggests that complexes are comprised of sets of opposite roles, like victim-perpetrator. One role is ego-syntonic, and the individual identifies with the characteristics. The other role is projected onto others. The constant re-experiencing of the complex, like Sisyphus's endless repetition of his journey up the mountain, is at the heart of problems in living. Thus, we see that the filter of the ego, including distortions that are locked in place as complexes, places limitations on the ability to become conscious of new experiences. This is the cause of mental suffering.

From Relational and Jungian Thought, we see that problems in living can arise as a result of the continual re-experiencing in a rigid, patterned manner due to projecting unconscious material onto the world and others. One's ability to have new experiences is eclipsed by the repetition of old experiences.

It is important to emphasize that from this perspective, we are born with an ability to know the other. It is only in the areas of injury that this capacity is damaged. Assumptions that others cannot be known may be a function of the degree of one's injury. From Fonagy and his colleagues' (2002) research, we can hypothesize that there is an additional pathway to mental difficulties. This is that, once again, due to early mental injury, a person may not have the ability to differentiate between their experiences and the subjective experiences of others. They experience the latter as their own but fail when they attempt to utilize their typical strategies to regulate these experiences.

3.2 How Therapy Helps From the Relational Perspective

From a contemporary psychoanalytic perspective, there are three aspects of treatment that help the client change and grow. These three interventions do not operate independently of each other; each drives the other. One intervention is insight/deconstruction. Through the process of inquiry (to be elaborated on in Chapter 6), a client can become aware of the patterns that have been operating outside of their ability to reflect on them (that is, as unimagined, unformulated, or unwelcome) and are restricting their capacity to have new, vitalizing experiences. This insight then gives the client options for resisting the pull into the old, dysfunctional pattern. By supporting the ability to verbally represent and reflect on qualia, the client can deconstruct them, which builds flexibility. Deconstruction is particularly useful in the process of exploring here-and-now experiences between the client and the therapist. By exploring how a client is distorting the present by repeating the past, focusing attention on the way the client experiences interactions with the therapist can help the client revise misconceptions and arrive at a new experience. Thus, for many Interpersonal Analysts and Therapists, deconstruction (which requires the ability to reflect on and verbalize) is an important aspect of activities aimed at promoting insight (Mann, 2009). But the Interpersonalists caution that insight alone is not sufficient to maintain changes in clients.

While insight and deconstruction contribute to the healing process, the fact that this activity is occurring in a specific kind of relationship receives greater emphasis in the Relational Schools of Psychoanalysis. One of the originating thinkers in the Relational School of Analysis, Stephen Mitchell (1988, 1997), gave careful consideration to the analytic relationship as an opportunity to stretch the rigid repetition of old patterns of experiencing the self and the other. The therapist consistently responds to the patient in a manner that is contrary to the client's expectations. Impact occurs when the analyst gets caught in the client's web of repeated experience. They fall into the client's expectations for how other people are. The therapist does not see this coming but instead realizes that they are in a situation that does not feel therapeutic. The therapeutic action resides in the therapist's efforts to find their way out of the situation (sometimes called an enactment). The therapist must present the client with a new experience of the self-with-other. "The analyst's . . . participation in new forms of interactions, enables the patient to encounter, name, and appreciate facets of his experience unknown before" (Mitchell, 1988, p. 289). The Boston Change Process Study Group (2010) has emphasized that this level of change can occur outside of the client's ability to reflect on it. It represents the implicit acquisition of new experience that stretches the old pattern far enough to allow the client to expect something different in the future.

Again, simply being a different person, responding to the clients' old patterns in new ways, is not, by itself, sufficient for change. Recall Stern's (1985) theory of development. The infant comes into the world with a mind that is naturally, automatically able to connect with another mind. Not only are they able to experience what-it's-like but there is a sense that they are happening to "me." The qualia, in response to attunement an adult caregiver is able to offer, begin to coalesce into patterned representations, or RIGs. New experiences have less power to change a RIG than early experiences. What this means in terms of therapy is that even though a therapist may provide a novel experience, that interaction is a late-comer in the representational process. Thus, there must be something more to cement a deep change. From a Relational Perspective, this something more is the connection between the minds of the therapist and client. This connection is referred to as the analytic field in the Interpersonal School (Lichtenberg, 2017), or intersubjectivity (Beebe et al., 2005) or "thirdness" (Benjamin, 2004) in the Intersubjective School.

The Boston Change Process Study Group (2010) has described the changes that occur as a result of this new connection. As suggested previously, during the process of inquiring into the areas of experience that generate insight, the changes on the subjective, implicit level are key. The study group has suggested that the client develops new forms of implicit relational knowledge by the "mutual knowing of what is in the other's mind" (Boston Change Process Study Group, 2010, p. 7). This connected knowing rearranges the mental actions of the client into progressively more coherent forms, which the group described as feeling like "a sudden qualitative change" (Boston Change Process Study Group, 2010, p. 7).

Recall Tronick and his colleagues' (1998) theory of infant development and his dyadically expanded states of consciousness hypothesis. He asserted that when an infant and mother are in the process of mutual regulation, they achieve a shared consciousness. This shared consciousness contains aspects of both parties' minds, and therefore adds information, cohesion, and complexity to both minds (more so the infant's, as the adult caregiver's mind is theoretically much more advanced in these areas than the infant's). It must be stressed that Tronick explains this process in physical terms. It is the brain that develops greater complexity and coherence.

Tronick et al. (1998) asserted that the same principle applies to psychotherapy. He and his co-writer (Cavelzani & Tronick, 2016) elaborated on this theory. Accepting inflexibility or lack of variability of one's self-organization as the root cause in problems in living, Cavelzani and Tronick suggested that this situation is resolved through the process of mutual regulation. Attunement, mis-attunement, and repair occur in moment-to-moment interactions between client and therapist, as well as over the course of a session or several sessions. Successful periods of mutual regulation lead to the dyadic expansion of consciousness for both the client and the therapist. Particularly for the client, the expanded shared consciousness reorganizes the client's consciousness, which affects their qualia beyond the therapeutic context. In addition, the newly expanded mind promotes the "reintegration and reconfiguration of already extant states of consciousness" (Tronick et al., 1998, p. 298).

For the Boston Change Process Study Group (2010), and one of the original members of the study group, Tronick, psychoanalytic change occurs as the direct result of the expansion that occurs when two minds connect. Likewise, the Interpersonal Analysts hold the connection between minds to be a primary mutative factor in therapy. They refer to this connection as the process that occurs in the analytic field. Old patterns break down and new ones are created as a result of the interaction between the therapist and the client (Peltz & Goldberg, 2013).

Galatzer-Levy (2009) has offered a model for how this change occurs. He used an analogy from quantum mechanics to illustrate his theory. Specifically, he suggested that psychoanalysis can use the activities of coupled oscillators within a field as a way of thinking about analytic action. It must be immediately noted that Galatzer-Levy discussed his theory in the context of mind-brain activity and appears to understand neurochemical processes to be key to the process. He nonetheless recognized mind as part of this process as well. One may choose to interpret his work through a cosmopsychist lens, such that the mind and the brain may correlate, without lapsing into a materialist ontology in which the brain is understood to be fundamental to the change process.

Galatzer-Levy (2009) discussed the fact that, in physical systems, there exists a process by which oscillators couple. An oscillator is a system that evinces dynamic stability, such as the "whirlpool" that was used in Chapter 1 to illustrate the nature of human consciousness. Coupling is the process of relating to or interacting with another oscillator in a field. The mere fact that oscillators become coupled is mutative:

> Each oscillator moves qualitatively differently from its movement when it was uncoupled. New patterns of motion appear that were not in evidence in the separate oscillators. . . . The coupling of oscillators . . . results in a new system with properties that go qualitatively beyond those of each component of the system. The system may allow processes in each component that could not occur in the components separately.
>
> (Galatzer-Levy, 2009, p. 991)

Put differently, the mutative action in therapy, according to Galatzer-Levy (2009), is understood to be the joining of the minds of the therapist and the client. The therapist's mind changes as a result of this activity. But, coupled oscillators may be asymmetrical in their relative strength: "initially the weaker oscillator appear(s) to be driven by the stronger" (Galatzer-Levy, 2009, p. 1002). While the notion of "stronger" and "weaker" are not appropriate to MCDT, it is important that the therapist's mind has greater flexibility in relation to the problems in living with which the client presents. This greater flexibility provides the opportunity for the therapist's mind to stretch the client's, allowing for new patterns in the latter.

Jungians may feel very much at home with this theory. Jung understood part of the work of therapy in this way: "a person [who] is a psychic system . . . enters into reciprocal reaction with another psychic system" (Jung, 1935/1966, para 1, cited in Evetts-Secker, 2010, p. 39). Evetts-Secker (2010) stressed the degree to which the analysts and analysand co-create meaning in the context of educational reciprocity. Of particular note here is the notion that psyches converge, and, in the process, both are enhanced.

These analytic accounts, taken together, suggest that several psychoanalysts as well as some Jungians posit that the connection of human minds is a transformative experience. The psychoanalysts stress that when one mind with a more highly developed degree of complexity and cohesiveness in relation to a given experience connects with a mind with a lesser degree of these attributes, the experience can stretch the latter and enhance its flexibility. This opens up the client to the possibility of experiencing in new ways.

For those who suffer as a result of another mind usurping their experience, the concept of intersubjectivity suggests that clients may be helped by being able to join with other minds while maintaining their own subjectivity and, hence sense of boundedness. This sense of self, as both separate, bounded, and unique and simultaneously connected, is important to MCDT, and thus will be explored at length in the next chapter.

3.3 Mind-Centered Depth Therapy (MCDT)

MCDT is built on the theoretical edifice constructed by the Relational Psychoanalysts, interpreted through the lens of cosmopsychism and extended mind theory. These views of mind have a significant degree of overlap. Recall the cosmopsychist view of the nature of mind as explicated by Shani (2015). Mind is qualia, or the sense of what it's like to be a particular person having a particular experience. An individual mind is a relatively stable pattern within the universal mind. That is, there is a typical way of perceiving and interpreting experience, which defines the individual. Although there is a high degree of stability for the patterns, they are, in fact, dynamic. This means that they are always in a state of flux, but that there is continuity even in the face of continual change. The stability of the patterns contributes to one of the fundamental aspects of mind: a sense of self or individuality, or separateness, and uniqueness. This sense of being a separate, unique unit can belie the fact that all minds are ultimately connected through their being parts of a single, shared phenomenal field. Because of the connection, minds combine and influence each other.

Now consider the thrust of the Psychoanalytic Theorists, as described previously. The human mind begins in connection and is shaped by the nature of the connection between an infant's and a caregiver's minds. The caregiver's subjective experiences influence the growing child's capacity to have subjective experiences; those experiences that can be shared can be reflected on, and thus developed. Those experiences that are not shared cannot be reflected on or elaborated on, and are continually and rigidly projected onto new situations. Optimally, the caregiver is able to share a wide range of experiences, and thus enhances the infant's repertoire of generalized experiences that influence the way that future situations are experienced. When this does not occur, the growing child has a paucity of capacity to experience, and enters into new situations by projecting expectations onto the new occurrences. This keeps the person locked in a cycle of repeating situations, even when those situations are associated with pain or dissatisfaction.

3.4 What *Is* It Like? The Nature of Qualia

Recall that in panpsychist circles, mind is qualia, or the experience of what-it's-like. MCDT is centered on helping clients change what-it's-like to have certain experiences, all the way up to and including what-it's-like to be who they are. We might benefit from clarifying a bit the kinds of phenomena that might be subsumed under what-it's-like.

Perhaps on the most obvious level, qualia include emotions and sensations. What it's like to bite into a ripe peach includes perhaps the smell of the peach, the sensation of the peach fuzz on the roof of your mouth, the texture of the pulp in your mouth, the wetness, and, of course, the flavor. What it's like to get cut off in traffic can include fear, anger, frustration. But both of these experiences include a host of other factors, depending on the individual and the event.

There are a number of continua on which the experience may fall, and the ways these factors interact with each other becomes important. For example, an experience can fall somewhere between pleasant and unpleasant, or morally/ethically good or bad. If Joe has the experience of being attracted to Sarah, he may find the experience pleasant but morally wrong. This would be a very different experience than Leo, who finds it pleasant but morally neutral or even good. Certainly, every continuum need not be implicated, and there are undoubtedly more than I can think of or list here. Some of them may include the degree to which a phenomenon may be relatively consistent or inconsistent with one's hopes, wishes, desires, motivations, intentions, etc. For example, the qualia associated with that ripe peach is going to depend on whether you were looking forward to it, or if you were craving cake and settled for a piece of fruit instead. The degree of familiarity or unfamiliarity may be an important part of the overall experience. One's associations and past experiences will influence the overall sense of what a phenomenon is like.

These various facets of mind are not separable. They cannot be independently measured. It is the interplay of each factor that creates an experience. The important point here is that, in MCDT, we are looking at our clients' qualia, with the understanding that any given quale is a complex, multifaceted phenomenon. Our job is not to simplify but to attempt to comprehend the wholeness and maintain the integrity of these complex experiences. We are attempting, to the best of our ability, to feel our way into what it's like to be this person, and what it's like to be this person who is, say, waking up every morning exhausted, with no motivation, and no sense of pleasure.

3.5 How Problems Arise From a MCDT Perspective

When these closely related views are melded, the combined theory is that problems in living center on the qualia, or sense of what it's like, that the client is continually re-experiencing. The individual suffers in some instances because they experience situations through misperception or the projection of past related situations, or because they are not able to register an experience at all.

In addition, MCDT posits that because the individual mind is both autonomous and unique, as well as connected, some problems in living arise when the individual fails to be able to discern both the boundedness and connectivity of minds. This will be explored at greater length in the next chapter. What is important to note here is that from a MCDT perspective, a subjective experience feels like "mine." In some cases, the individual's subjective experience is a combination of what they have experienced previously in combination with the current context. The experience is not identical to a past experience, but is consistent with it. These experiences are often intersubjective. As we have seen, in other cases there is no admittance of an other; instead, the past is recapitulated to the detriment of the individual. I refer to these experiences as "endogenous." In yet other cases, the individual may not contribute to an intersubjective experience, but instead contaige someone else's subjectivity. The term "exogenous" may apply to these kinds of subjective experiences. Thus, the ability to open up or expand patterns of experience, as well as the ability to discern if one's current subjective experience is endogenous or exogenous, becomes highly important.

The goal of MCDT is to help clients change their minds or increase the complexity and cohesiveness in order to engage in and reflect on, and hence elaborate on, new experiences, as well as identify the source of a subjective experience. In many cases, this means expanding rigid mental patterns that inhibit one from taking in new information from the environment and experiencing new qualia, but instead projecting expectations based on past experiences onto current experiences. In some cases, it means helping individuals learn to discern subtle differences between qualia that are the result of their own expectations and processes, and those that are the result of contagions from another mind.

3.6 The Mutative Nature of Therapy From a MCDT Perspective

The Relational, Interpersonal, and Intersubjective Theories of the ways in which therapy changes a person posit three aspects of psychotherapy that contribute to growth: insight/deconstruction, a new type of interaction that can update relational representations, and an increase in the complexity and coherence of the brain structure as the result of being in a state of mutual regulation with the therapist. Infant researchers and psychoanalytic theorists often maintain an allegiance to the physicalist model that was explained in Chapter 1: that is, mind is an epiphenomenon of the brain. Therefore, the site of change that is important is ultimately the brain.

From a panpsychist perspective, understanding mental processes as the result of neurochemical processes is an unjustifiable leap. Panpsychist philosophers (Goff, 2019) agree that the shift from purely physical processes to qualia, or feeling what it's like, has not been sufficiently explained by the physicalist ontology. The explanations always come down to a magical moment in which that which has physical properties becomes something that does not have any physical properties. Based on this view, the notion that the change in subjectivity that results from two people being in attunement cannot be adequately explained in terms of the brain or neurochemical processes.

A cosmopsychist and extended mind theory interpretation of the mutative aspect of therapy, as described by the Relational Psychoanalysts, is that it is the *minds* of the therapist and the client that directly connect; there is no need to posit the exchange of quantum particles or refer to a mysterious process through which visual and auditory stimuli trigger a physical process that renders the non-physical qualia. It is the *purely mental* mutual regulation that leads to the dyadic expansion, or the extended mind. The bi-laterally extended mind has many qualities of both minds. This allows both participants to experience enhanced mental cohesiveness and complexity that can endure beyond the period of connection. It also explains how each comes to know the mind of the other, or, in other words, to intuitively acquire information about some of the mental processes and content of the other.

Like Relational Psychotherapy, MCDT posits that insight/deconstruction is highly important to help promote change. In MCDT, the insight is aimed at helping clients become aware of their typical patterns, especially the degree of rigidity of the kinds of qualia they re-experience, as well as begin to imagine that there are qualia that they have thus far not experienced but could. The conversation between the client and the therapist supports the client in verbally representing experience, and through this process the qualia can be reflected upon. Those experiences that can be reflected upon and represented are less likely to be projected onto future situations, but can contribute to new contexts in order to render new experiences.

The relationship between the client and the therapist is an avenue to help clients access experiences that were previously rejected because they threatened important ties. The therapist works to share and validate experiences that the client learned were dangerous to relationships. Thus, this form of intervention is especially helpful in working through unwelcome qualia. The new kind of relationship that the MCDT therapist works to establish is one in which the client's subjectivity is the central concern. A client will not enter into a mutually created mind-field unless they feel sufficiently safe to do so. Safety means that they will not disappear in the field; they will not be overwhelmed by the therapist's mind. Likewise, they will be supported and understood. It is absolutely necessary for the therapist to center on what it's like to be this other person, to be able to hold the client's mind in their mind. Likely, the client has either never been offered or has rejected this kind of relationship. Thus, the MCDT therapist must adjust their presentation, the level or degree of mental connection, in accordance with what the individual client needs and can tolerate. This requires the use of clinical intuition on the part of the therapist (as will be explored in Chapter 6).

The third element of change in MCDT is the mental connection. The theory of what causes problems in living suggests that therapists who work from this perspective are actively engaged in moment-to-moment shifts to help clients regulate into new patterns of enmindedness. In relational terms, the minds of the therapist and the client extend bi-directionally to form a process of mutual sharing. From the perspective of MCDT, there is no need to do anything to extend the mind in order to make a connection: the connection is there. The mind in which we all participate is an ontological connection. We only need to open up to it, or, in different words, to surrender to it. We invite our clients to relax their minds to feel the connection with us. In widening to each other, we are both opening to a new experience. We are opening our minds. The experience of the connection allows our clients' minds to become more coherent and complex, to directly experience something new. While a great deal of this action is purposeful, a great deal of the activity takes place on an implicit level.

An individual mind can be altered by combining with another individual mind. The combination is achieved through the therapist opening up to experience the client's qualia. At the same time, the client experiences the therapist's mind as well, although this is an asymmetrical exchange. The greater the degree of the therapist understanding what it's like to be the client, the more effective the connection will be between minds. According to analytic developmental theory, the ability to share experience is an important aspect of what experiences one is able to have in the future. As the therapist is able to share more and more of the client's previously truncated experiences, the more and more the client will be able to elaborate on them and have new experiences. The client accomplishes this without losing the integrity and articulation in their sense of self, and simultaneously realize their embeddedness in the unitary whole and connection with all other aspects of the whole. This allows them to differentiate between the endogenous mind and the exogenous mind. Thus, the MCDT therapist attempts to work by means of the connection between minds so that the client can have a broader range of experiences than they have previously enjoyed.

It must be immediately noted that in the experience, this new state is felt, due to the nature of mind, as "mine," as happening to me. That is, both participants in the shared mind-process are experiencing this phenomenon as their own subjective state. In order to be helpful to the client, the MCDT therapist must have developed a high degree of self-awareness so that they are able to discern which subjective experiences in this state are part of their own repertoire, and thus discern what the client is likely contributing to the interaction. This process is closely tied to clinical intuition, which we will see is an important aspect of the MCDT treatment approach.

In terms of the client, one recurrent problem that may contribute to their problems in living may be due to the fact that, rather than a shared mind-state, they are overwhelmed by another's mind. This happens automatically with a low degree of awareness. When the caregiver does not adequately attend to the infant's mind, the infant does not develop the capacity to recognize their own mind. These clients may present with a great deal of dysphoric affect—anxiety, most notably. The feeling is not consistent with other aspects of their internal state, so it feels strange, even while it feels like "theirs." For example, a client may be feeling highly anxious about a project at work, when they are typically confident in relation to their job. Upon close inspection, it becomes clear that they have contaiged the feelings. Perhaps from a colleague with whom they are collaborating on the project. In some cases, a client easily contaiges the ambient anxiety that pervades their social environment. In such cases, MCDT can help by giving these clients the ability to identify the source of their subjective experience and to regulate the connection with or inflow of other minds. Thus, we see that change in MCDT comes as the result of the minds of the therapist and the client connecting, and the client developing the ability to connect and disconnect with other minds with greater awareness and choice.

3.7 Practice Implications

The practice implications for this chapter are quite consistent with the implications noted in Chapter 4. As we will explore, helping clients identify the source of qualia, and how to metabolize the information differentially, is an important part of MCDT. This means helping clients to hold a sense of self that is simultaneously independent and bounded, as well as a sense of self that is connected and permeable. This is the focus of the next chapter.

3.8 Conclusion

MCDT is based on the view of mind proffered by researchers and analysts as well as philosophers of mind. It begins with the premise that the human mind develops as a result of being connected to a more cohesive, complex mind. When the latter does not share experiences with the infant, those experiences cannot be developed or elaborated on. Instead, they remain stuck; the person then projects these experiences onto new situations. The kinds of problems that lead clients to seek psychotherapy are the results of this developmental process; the repertoire of the kinds of experiences an individual has is highly restricted. The template for how they perceive and experience life is inflexible. In other cases, because the caregiver could not reflect the infant's subjective state, but instead imposed their own onto the child, the individual is left unable to differentiate between their own and others' subjectivity.

From the psychoanalytic perspective, there are three interventions that correct for these problems. The first is insight/deconstruction. In reflecting on and verbalizing past and present interactions, one perceives how one structures experiences in ways that contribute to problems in living. This opens the possibility for engaging and experiencing in new ways. The second mutative aspect of Relational Psychotherapy is through providing the client with a new kind of relationship. By falling into the client's pull to recapitulate relationships in dysfunctional ways, and then by finding a way out of the situation to create a new relational experience, clients' patterns begin to loosen. But perhaps the most impactful change strategy in Relational Analysis is the connection of minds. Through the kind of attunement that spurs development in infancy, the therapist can stretch the client's mental structures to help them expand their mental templates to become more complex and cohesive.

3.9 Key Points

- When caregivers are able to mentally share experiences with an infant, the infant is able to reflect on and elaborate on those experiences. This gives the experience a degree of flexibility, so that future situations can be experienced with a degree of plasticity. When caregivers are not able to mentally share experiences with infants, the infant cannot reflect on that experience, and thus the experience becomes rigidified and projected onto future situations.
- It is this mental rigidity and projection that lead to problems in living.
- There is another pathway to pathology: when the caregiver imposes their own mental experience on the child, and the child experiences this situation as alien but understands it to be their own. Because they mistake the source of such experiences, they are unable to regulate them.
- To resolve mental difficulties, therapists must help their clients increase their mental flexibility as well as discern the source of qualia.
- There are three ways to intervene with clients to help them overcome mental difficulties. The first is to help the client reflect on and verbalize patterns that are associated with their difficulties. The second is to stretch those patterns by forming a new kind of relationship with the client. The third is by co-creating a shared mental state with the client.
- This shared mental state is the foundation of clinical intuition.

3.10 References

Beebe, B., Knoblauch, S., Rustin, J., Sorter, D., Jacobs. T. J., & Pally, R. (2005). *Forms of intersubjectivity in infant research and adult treatment.* Other Press.

Benjamin, J. (2004). Beyond doer and done to: An intersubjective view of thirdness. *The Psychoanalytic Quarterly, 73*(1), 5–46. https://doi.org/10.1002/j.2167-4086.2004.tb00151.x

Boston Change Process Study Group. (2010). *Change in psychotherapy: A unifying paradigm.* W. W. Norton & Co.

Cavelzani, A., & Tronick, E. (2016). Dyadically expanded states of consciousness and therapeutic change in the interaction between analyst and patient. *Psychoanalytic Dialogues*, 26(5), 599–615. https://doi.org/10.1080/10481885.2016.1214478

Cooper, A. (1995/2015). The detailed inquiry. In M. Lionells, J. Fiscalini, C. H. Mann, & D. B. Stern (Eds.), *Handbook of interpersonal psychoanalysis* (pp. 679–693). Routledge.

Evetts-Secker, J. (2010). Initiating psychological education. In M. Stein (Ed.), *Jungian psychoanalysis: Working in the spirit of C. G. Jung* (pp. 38–44). Open Court.

Fonagy, P., Gergely, G., Jurist, E. L., & Target, M. (2002). *Affect regulation, mentalization, and the development of the self.* Other Press.

Galatzer-Levy, R. M. (2009). Good vibrations: Analytic process as coupled oscillations. *International Journal of Psychoanalysis*, 99, 983–1007. https://doi.org/10.1111/j.1745-8315.2009.00188.x

Goff, P. (2019). *Galileo's error: Foundations for a new science of consciousness.* Pantheon.

Hall, C. S., & Nordby, V. J. (1973). *A primer of Jungian psychology.* Meridian.

Jung, C. G. (1935/1966). Principles of practical psychotherapy (R. F. C. Hull, Trans.). In H. Read et al. (Series Eds.), *The collected works of C. G. Jung* (Vol. 16, part B,). Princeton University Press. (Original work published in 1935).

Lichtenberg, J. (2017). Forward. In S. M. Katz (Ed.), *Contemporary psychoanalytic field theory: Stories, dreams, and metaphor* (pp. ix–xii). Routledge.

Mann, C. H. (2009). The goals of interpersonal psychoanalysis. In M. Lionells, J. Fiscalini, C. H. Mann, & D. B. Stern (Eds.), *Handbook of interpersonal psychoanalysis* (pp. 555–567). Routledge.

Mitchell, S. A. (1988). *Relational concepts in psychoanalysis: An integration.* Harvard University Press.

Mitchell, S. A. (1993). *Hope and dread in psychoanalysis.* Basic Books.

Mitchell, S. A. (1997). *Influence and autonomy in psychoanalysis.* The Analytic Press.

Peltz, R., & Goldberg, P. (2013). Field conditions: Discussion of Donnel B. Stern's *Field Theory in Psychoanalysis. Psychoanalytic Dialogues*, 23, 660–666. https://doi.org/10.1080/10481885.2013.851553

Perry, J. W. (1970). Emotions and object relations. *Journal of Analytical Psychology*, 47(1), 1–12. https://doi.org/10.1111/j.1465-5922.1970.00001.x

Shani, I. (2015). Cosmopsychism: A holistic approach to the metaphysics of experience. *Philosophical Papers*, 44, 389–437. https://doi.org/10.1080/05568641.2015.1106709

Stern, D. N. (1985). *The interpersonal world of the infant: A view from psychoanalysis and developmental psychology.* Basic Books.

Stolorow, R. D., & Atwood, G. E. (1994). Toward a science of human experience. In R. Stolorow, G. Atwood, & B. Brandchaft (Eds.), *The intersubjective perspective* (pp. 15–30). Rowman & Littlefield.

Tronick, E., Bruschweiler-Stern, N., Harrison, A. M., Lyons-Ruth, K., Morgan, A. C., Nahum, J. P., Sander, L., & Stern, D. (1998). Dyadically expanded states of consciousness and the process of therapeutic change. *Infant Mental Health Journal*, 19(3), 290–299.

Vesey-McGrew, P. (2010). Getting on top of thought and behavior patterns. In M. Stein (Ed.), *Jungian psychoanalysis: Working in the spirit of C. G. Jung* (pp. 14–21). Open Court.

Differentiating Sources of Qualia and Experiencing the Self as Individual and the Self as Connected

4

My client's sense of self—what-it's-like to be them—is at the center of a mind-centered depth therapeutic approach. As we will see in this chapter, the sense of self is closely tied to one's ability to differentiate between and work with different sources of qualia. Qualia can arise as the result of the process of experiencing life in a repetitive way. I call this endogenous, for it is we who are reproducing the same experience over and over. Likewise, as we have seen in the developmental literature, and especially in the Interpersonal Theory of Development, we can contaige affect (and I assert other qualia) from other people and/or the environment. If I contaige qualia easily, but see it as my own, I will have problems with how I experience myself and the world.

If I keep generating the same small set of qualia because I distort situations and see them as "just like" what happened in the past, I will have problems with how I experience myself and the world. Thus, it is important in MCDT that I am able to experience myself as a bounded individual, with full ownership and responsibility for the qualia I generate. The sense of self as bounded incorporates such therapeutic concerns as self-awareness, identity, self-esteem, and agency.

Equally, I must be able to have a sense of self as connected to others and the world, able to take in qualia from sources external to me. This sense of self is associated with treatment foci such as our appreciation of the subjectivity of the other and our ability to use and regulate exogenous qualia.

DOI: 10.4324/9781003090816-6

The ability to discern and manage the sources of qualia will impact my sense of self. Therefore, helping clients appropriately identify what is "theirs" and what is "not theirs," along with the ability to see the self as both individual, bounded, and unique, as well as the ability to see the self as connected and permeable, are important foci of MCDT.

4.1 Sources of Qualia

We can look at three sources of qualia. First, an individual may auto-generate a sense of what a situation is like. Second, a person can be involved in an intersubjective relationship in which two (or more) people are co-creating qualia with each other. Third, a person can take in qualia from an external source. It must be stressed that this division is heuristic; it is not possible to neatly slice up the source of a given individual's experience. In all cases, there are differing amounts of self-generated, co-generated, and other-generated aspects of an experience. But I assert that, for the sake of mental well-being, we can benefit from this understanding. Helping clients distinguish which of these three sources of qualia are most relevant in a given situation allows us to help clients learn how to optimally use and/or regulate qualia to overcome their problems in living.

The analyst Neil Altman (2020) echoes the work of the panpsychists, who identify the self as a dynamic pattern. Altman refers to the self as a strange attractor. That is, what-it's-like to be me tends to be attracted toward a specific form of organization; in the terminology developed in this book, we each have a relatively stable pattern of perceiving and interpreting phenomena. When a new situation is encountered, it evokes old unformulated or unwelcome experiences that exist outside of our ability to reflect on or symbolically represent. One's current experience can thus be largely (albeit not exclusively) produced by endogenous processes that recapitulate the past. For example, if my parents scoffed at me for wanting to pursue a creative career, when I am called upon to participate in a creative project at work, I may feel a great deal of anxiety. This situation was stressed in the last chapter as one of two sources for problems in living: individuals auto-generate painful qualia, often distorting the way the current situation is perceived. These experiences may also be termed the "endogenous mind" or "endogenous qualia."

As we have seen, the Relational Analysts and Developmental Researchers have demonstrated that people can also have intersubjective experiences. Here, the individual maintains their subjectivity while simultaneously entering into a mind-field with another person. The two will co-create a new experience that is not the product of either mind alone but is comprised of two minds coming together to create something that is familiar to both, even while new. This requires a flexible mind. This experience, as noted by the Boston Change Process Study Group (2010), is a very pleasant, enlivening experience. Think about a deep conversation you had with a close friend. You could finish each other's sentences. You felt completely understood. New ideas were emerging out of the shared experience. The experience left you feeling really good.

A third experience is when one person contaiges the experiences of another person. These experiences feel like "I" am the one having this experience even though this is not consistent with what may be typical for me. For example, you may be experiencing anxiety about an upcoming vacation, but you cannot identify why. You have traveled previously. Those experiences were very successful. Yet this time you are apprehensive. You keep checking your suitcase, racking your brain to figure out what you could possibly be forgetting. You might wonder why you are doing this to yourself. Is it a premonition? Why can't you calm yourself down? All the self-talk in the world does not quell the anxiety. It may be that your friend, with whom you are going on vacation, has a great deal of difficulty traveling. They have not shared their difficulty with you, but nonetheless they are experiencing their usual anxiety as you prepare for the trip. You may be contaiging or internalizing your friend's anxiety. As we saw in Chapter 3, this concept is central to the work of Sullivan (1954/1970) and other Interpersonal Analysts (Crastnopol, 1995/2009). Other terms for this type of experience are "exogenous mind" and "exogenous qualia."

In the analytic literature, the source of qualia is related to one's sense of self. The analysts stress the value of experiencing oneself as bounded, individual, and unique. Even though the analytic literature stresses that these characteristics are the result of connected minds, there is no mention of the importance of helping clients recognize the source of exogenous qualia. This is even the case among Interpersonal Analysts, for whom exogenous anxiety is the root cause of all problems in living. The Transpersonal Psychologists, elaborating on the work of Jung, recognize that one must be able to experience the self as connected. But they also do not discuss the therapeutic value of helping clients differentiate the source of qualia in order to use the experience for optimal well-being.

4.2 The Self in the Relational Psychoanalytic Literature: Bounded and Separate

The Relational Analytic Schools understand a healthy sense of self to include the boundedness of the individual. The self has an outside and an inside, and the failure to experience the separation of the two is seen as pathological. According to Weigmann (2013), "neurological disorders, notably schizophrenia, can . . . cause people to lose the feeling of 'self' and to live instead with the impression that other people or unknown forces are controlling their thoughts and actions" (p. 765).

The developmental literature supports this basic contention: a sense of self as a bounded, individual agent is necessary for psychological well-being. Daniel Stern (1985) emphasized that a sense of core self, which emerges at about two to three months old, is comprised of four experiences:

> *self-agency* [is] authorship of one's own actions and nonauthorship of the actions of others . . . *self-coherence*, [or] having a sense of being a non-fragmented, physical whole with boundaries and a locus of integrated action, both while moving (behaving) and when still; *self-affectivity*, experiencing patterned inner qualities of feeling (affects) that belong with other experiences of self; and . . . *self-history*, having the sense of enduring, of a continuity with one's own past . . . and can change even while remaining the same. The infant notes regularities in the flow of events.
>
> (Stern, 1985, p. 71)

All of these aspects of self-experience are tied to the self as an individual, bounded entity. You are the author of your experiences. In other words, there is the suggestion that understanding all qualia to be endogenous is healthy, and experiencing the porousness of the self—the feeling that one's experiences have a source outside of the self—is pathological.

There are prescribed ways of experiencing one's individuality that underlie well-being throughout the analytic literature. One important experience is the capacity to reflect on this individualized self (Fonagy et al., 2002). But while this individuality is demonstrated to be, in fact, the product of connectedness, it is not equally stressed that one have and reflect on the self-experience of permeability. Put differently, the ability for a client to discern the differences between those subjective experiences that are part of their relatively stable pattern of perceiving and interpreting experiences (their bounded self), and those that emanate from or are transmitted by others (their permeable self), has thus far not been stressed in the treatment literature. This may be due to the enduring view that a sense of self-as-permeable is associated with pathological states.

Yet the connected nature of minds and the recognition of the existence of exogenous qualia is highly valued for therapists in the Relational literature. The

Relational Analysts stress the role of intersubjectivity in the treatment process. But, as we can see, with appropriate self-awareness, the analyst can titrate out their contribution to the interpersonal field and, thus, ascertain the nature of the client's influence on their subjectivity. Aron (1996) was an early advocate for recognizing the role of mutual influence in the treatment process. He referenced the "realm of the between" and the "transitional space" between the analyst and the analysand. He stated, "we constantly influence one another, consciously and unconsciously, and in this way patient and analyst weave the complex tapestry of the transference-countertransference; through negotiation they reach a meeting of the minds" (Aron, 1996, p. 69). Aron stated that the therapist must remain aware of how their subjectivity is being influenced by the jointly constructed space between themselves and the client. In a similar vein, Mitchell (1997) discussed Ehrenberg's work (1992), noting that for the latter, it is her shifting "sense of self in the presence of the patient . . . [that allows her] to generate hypotheses about the patient" (Mitchell, 1997, p. 149). There is an explicit recognition here that the "self" of the therapist is permeable, and that they must remain aware of specifically how the interaction with the client is affecting their own subjectivity. Again, the Relationalists speak in terms of co-created experience, but they also suggest that this co-created experience can give the therapist insight into the client's subjectivity. The therapist remains aware of what is endogenous and discerns which subjective experiences they are having, which in fact emanate in some way from the client.

The work of Aron, Mitchell, and other Relational Analysts was a revolution in analytic thought, and certainly of monumental importance to the development of analytic practice. Perhaps it is now time to take the next step in this line of thinking. Just as the therapist must be aware of how they are influencing the client and how the client is influencing them, the client may find psychological benefit in the ability to apprehend and reflect on how the therapist—as well as others in their lives—impacts their subjective experience. The suggestion here is that there is a meliorative effect to people having a self-experience of the diffuse nature of the self-boundary, and that are able to distinguish those subjective experiences that constitute their patterned ways of perceiving and interpreting experience (what is "theirs") and how this is influenced by others in specific interactions (what they are "catching" from other), as well as by the larger environment. It is not currently part of the Relational Treatment Process to help clients develop the ability to apprehend or reflect on experiences of the permeability of the self-boundary, and that sometimes they are experiencing exogenous qualia.

I am suggesting here that the way one manages endogenous qualia is different from the way one manages exogenous qualia. In addition, as will become clear in the following discussion of intuition, qualia are associated with information. Knowing where qualia come from helps us discern helpful information about a situation that may aid us in making more adaptive decisions. In other words, the ability to see the self as both bounded and permeable is an important aspect of mental/emotional well-being and interpersonal interactions.

Brown (2017) argues that Relational Analysis is an important step forward in the evolution of analytic thought. He stresses, however, that the theories retain a philosophical commitment to materialism. He calls for a "postrelational" turn that incorporates a post-Jungian interpretation of a transpersonal approach to clinical practice. It is in this post-Jungian literature that we see the full expression of the clinical benefit of clients experiencing the connected nature of the self.

4.3 Jung's Treatment of the Self

Jung, as we have noted, breaks the unconscious into the personal unconscious and the collective unconscious. The former is comprised of repressed material as well as subliminal material that has not risen to the level of consciousness. These contents are the result of life experiences. The collective unconscious is a set of categories, or archetypes, that are inherited in a genetic sense. According to Jung, the unconscious material is in a complimentary or compensatory relationship with conscious material. The totality formed by the conscious and unconscious is the self. In this way, he differentiates the conscious ego from the self. The self is an archetype of an all-embracing wholeness, which Jung identifies with God and Christ at various points in his work *Aion: Researches into the Phenomenology of the Self* (1959/1978). This brings Jungian thought squarely in the arena of valuing the self as connected. This point is made more clearly in inspecting the goal of Jungian therapy.

For Jung, therapy helps to bring the personal unconscious into the consciousness, thereby altering the proportion of personal to collective unconscious (less personal unconscious, thus relatively more collective unconscious). It seems that there is an implication here that the personal unconscious promotes a more rigid repetition of endogenous qualia. On the other hand, the collective unconscious is associated with greater permeability of the self and thus the ability to function in connection with the world. Thus, the goal of treatment for Jung was to help the individual apprehend the connection between themselves and the wider human collective.

4.4 The Self in the Transpersonal Approach: Connected and Porous

As the previous quotes from Weigmann (2013) and Stern (1985) reveal, the analytic literature on psychopathology stresses that a sense that one is not responsible for their subjective states may be associated with schizophrenia and other abnormal conditions. The Transpersonal Psychotherapists, who describe a significant Jungian influence, see it otherwise. Within Transpersonal Psychology there is an understanding that it is the sense of self as separate that contributes to psychological distress.

The limitations of the approach in traditional psychology to focus on the self-as-bounded is lamented by Louchakova and Lucas (2007); they noted that traditional "[t]herapeutic techniques . . . are prone to strengthen the coping-in-isolation for a masterful, bounded, empty self . . . at the expense of an engaged, warm, interrelational, and meaningful human life" (p. 120). The authors call instead for the adoption of an awareness of the "indivisible continuum of life as a therapeutic premise" (Louchakova & Lucas, 2007, p. 126). To be sure, they are largely centered on the end of this continuum at which the individual experiences oneness with a timeless, spaceless, all-encompassing phenomenon. Nonetheless, as the term "continuum" implies, the sense of self-as-permeable includes an awareness of one's connection with all phenomena subsumed within the entirety. Thus, the work of Louchakova and Lucas approaches the suggestion put forward here: helping clients directly experience the permeability of the self-boundary, to apprehend and reflect on the influence of the "not self" on the self, has positive mutative value in therapy.

For Transpersonal Therapists, the psychological benefits of recognizing the diffuse nature of the boundary between the self and the other—the ontological connectedness of everything—and thus the understanding that one can have experiences that are not self-authored is in fact a central construct. The emphasis in this literature and practice is on the results of one having a direct experience in altered states of consciousness with a "larger, even infinite, Being, Consciousness, or Mind, along with the recognition of one's own transpersonal identity and link with this boundless Mind" (Walsh & Vaughan, 2018, p. 1). As this description makes clear, the focus is on the awareness of connectedness with something far beyond the other person with whom one is interacting, and thus the permeability of the self-boundary.

Transpersonal Therapy brings the act of purposefully contaiging another's qualia as a source of clinical information into the forefront. Of note is

Rowan's (2002) observation about the client-therapist relationship that is common among Relational Therapists. This is that the therapeutic relationship requires a shift in the self-boundary of the therapist so that they can experience "interbeing . . . linking . . . communion . . . and so forth" (Rowan, 2002, p. 102). He stressed the role of therapists' intuition in the treatment process. In accessing intuition, he is clear that the therapist is receiving exogenously generated information: "at this level intuition is essentially seen as coming from a source other than one's own isolated self. Action must be taken to open oneself up to this source" (Rowan, 2002, p. 106).

As much as Transpersonal Psychology places stress on expanding the sense of self beyond ego-identification, Transpersonal Therapists consistently recognize the necessity for clients to hold both a sense of self as bounded (the author of endogenous qualia) as well as a sense of self as permeable (the recipient of exogenously generated qualia). Although Scotton (1985) referred to therapy that is aimed at helping clients to overcome "wounds, problems, or developmental arrests of the individual" (p. 57), he labeled this level of treatment as reductive. Nonetheless, he noted that patients who engage in Transpersonal Psychotherapy must be willing to work at the reductive level, and therapists who conduct this brand of treatment must "obtain and maintain a firm grounding in psychotherapy. If one cannot do good reductive psychotherapy, one cannot do half the job" (Scotton, 1985, p. 61). He argued that productive Transpersonal Psychotherapy must manage this twin focus.

Vaughan (1979b), a pioneer in the development of Transpersonal Therapy, likewise recognized the necessity to work with clients on issues that are associated with the endogenous mind as well as the exogenous mind. Vaughan outlined a non-linear progression in the therapeutic process for the unfolding of the senses of the self. An important part of this work is attending to well-being at the level of the ego. The work includes enhancing ego-strength, positive self-esteem, and the capacity for self-validation. She noted, "As one begins to identify and own feelings, thoughts, and previously rejected or projected parts of the self, one can assume responsibility for who one is and for the consequences of the choices one has made" (Vaughan, 1979b, p. 106). In therapeutic progression, the client moves through disidentification, wherein "While owning that one has a body, feelings, thoughts and points of view, one recognizes that one is no-thing" (Vaughan, 1979b, p. 106). In the final stage of self-transcendence:

> One no longer experiences oneself as totally isolated, but as part of something larger, inherently connected, and related to everything. The realization that one exists as a web of mutually conditioned relationships

and that one is absolutely connected with all of existence may be . . . the next step in human evolution.

(Vaughan, 1979b, p. 106)

Vaughan's (1979b) and Scotton's (1985) observations may be interpreted to suggest that psychological health and well-being are associated with an integrated view of the self as simultaneously bounded and permeable: the author of endogenous qualia and the recipient of exogenous qualia. From the perspective of MCDT, the ability to identify the source of qualia becomes an important treatment objective on the road to learning how to regulate qualia in some circumstances, and appropriately use the information that is associated with the experience in all circumstances.

4.5 Religion and Spirituality and Psychotherapy

This discussion of Transpersonal Psychology may raise the question as to whether the Transpersonal Perspective that a healthy individual experiences the self as connected crosses a boundary from psychotherapy to spirituality and religion. This has become an important question in the last several decades. There are several studies that confirm two things: first, psychologists tend to be uncomfortable discussing religion and spirituality in therapy, and second, a person's sense of connectedness is correlated with a sense of well-being and greater life-satisfaction (see, for example, Brown et al., 2013). To this end, there has been a growing trend in psychotherapy to incorporate techniques that are traditionally associated with religious traditions. Among these are mindfulness practices and centering prayer.

Here, we are interested in the sense of self as connected. Therefore, I am going to bracket the conversation on religion and focus on spirituality. A number of writers agree that spirituality is difficult to define. Yet, there is good amount of agreement in the literature that spirituality is associated with a relationship with or an experience of connectedness to something beyond the self. This is not necessarily deistic. In some of the literature, this experience is termed "self-transcendence." Self-transcendence has been correlated in a number of studies with both well-being and mental health. In any event, the work of Robin Brown (2020) represents a large step toward the need to incorporate issues of spirituality into analytic practice.

I personally find it very interesting that helping clients develop a sense of self as individual, unique, and bounded is widely considered an appropriate area of exploration in psychotherapy. Yet helping clients develop a sense of self as connected and permeable is a different area of practice; it belongs to the realm of spirituality. What I am suggesting here is that the sense of self is a highly important construct in psychotherapy. Understanding and experiencing the sense of self as simultaneously bounded and individual, as well as connected and permeable, is an important area of focus for mental health professionals, regardless of traditional boundaries between spirituality and psychotherapy.

4.6 Mind-Centered Depth Therapy (MCDT) and the Senses of the Self

A mind-centered depth approach to therapy combines the work of the Relational Analysts and Jungian and post-Jungian psychologists. The result is the assertion that a healthy sense of self requires that one be able to hold a sense of self that is simultaneously individual, unique, and bounded, as well as connected and porous. Indeed, based on my clinical experience, I have come to see that the central conflict in human life is the reality of this twin nature. It seems that we move up and down the continuum, rarely satisfied with where we are: we want to be honored more as the unique being who we are, we want our subjective experience to be valued, we want to make choices for ourselves and follow our own inner strivings, and we want to be able to impact our environments in line with our will. And yet, we need others to see and honor our uniqueness. We want to be understood by others, accepted by others, and we want to be like others; we need to be validated by others. Others' perspectives impact us on every level, and we require this impact in order to be fully human. This is not a "spiritual" issue; it is a human issue.

Thus, a healthy sense of self in MCDT includes objectives linked to the sense of self as an individual and as connected. In terms of our individuality, there are several areas that are important. As has been stressed throughout this book, a sense of self as an individual is premised on self-awareness; this means the ability to identify and then reflect on and symbolize our qualia. This means to be able to "catch" discrete qualia in the moment, as well as to be able to apprehend tendencies to repeat certain experiences.

Healthy individuality also requires that we must have a clear and relatively consistent, although complex, identity: we can flexibly adapt to a context without losing a sense of authenticity. A healthy identity includes a sense of self as valuable (self-esteem), with awareness of the virtues that we strive to incorporate into our character and characteristics with which we identify.

I have seen many clients who identify themselves as what they do, or what they have, or what they want, unable to see themselves in terms of virtues or personal characteristics: they cannot identify as honest, or dependable, etc. It also means being able to own our weaknesses, and non-defensively admit to our character flaws and mistakes. We must balance the twin capacities to accept ourselves as we are and continue our efforts to improve.

Self-as-individual includes a healthy sense of agency. This means that we know that we have an effect on the world and take responsibility for our actions. It means that we are able to determine if acting on our qualia is an effective option (exercising will), or if regulating our qualia is the best course for the situation. We also appreciate the limits of our control and power, and consistently honor the agency of others, able to find a balance between the needs and desires of the self and the other.

There are people who do not see the effect they have on the world; they do not believe that they are able to have any kind of impact on their own lives or the lives of others. I see this manifesting in clients as profound inconsideration of others, unaware that their actions affect other people. I also see difficulties with agency in clients who believe that their experiences are the result of forces beyond their control. They see their suffering as "just the way my brain works" or because they have a specific diagnosis. The problem with this is when they name their diagnoses as if this has happened to them and that there is nothing that they can do about it. They believe they may be happy one day after something changes, with no ability to understand that it is they who must make the change.

As both agency and identity suggest, people also function better when they understand and appreciate the degree to which they are connected to other people and the world as a whole. As noted previously, awareness of connection means that you can reflect on the degree to which your experience is being colored by the experiences of others. This includes the physical as well as the social environment. Not only are we aware of how our experiences are impacted by external phenomena, but connection also requires that we experience our effect on others.

This ability to feel the self as connected requires, perhaps counterintuitively for some, that we value the differences between ourselves and others. The infant researcher and psychoanalyst Beatrice Beebe and her colleagues (2005) have studied the connection between minds and have arrived at the conclusion that just as important as it is for us to experience the same thing together, it is equally important to appreciate the degree to which our mind and that of another are different. A healthy sense of connectedness means that we are fully aware of the fact that the person with whom we are linked is a separate center of subjectivity. It is too easy to assume similarity and then perceive what we expect to see. In this circumstance, we are not actually able to reflect on our connection to another; we are projecting our experiences onto them, distorting the impact of our ontological linking. Connection is not limited to those moments when we are having a common experience, but equally includes valuing all of the times that we are having different experiences as well.

The sense of self-as-connected brings the twin experiences of humility in the face of being but a tiny part of something much greater, and the aplomb that accompanies being an aspect of the universe. Some clients find that their awareness of connectedness brings a sense of greater meaning.

The senses of self as individual and connected are, as suggested previously, intimately tied to one's capacity to recognize the source of qualia and appropriately use this information to regulate the experience. In MCDT, an objective of treatment is to help clients distinguish whether an experience is endogenous or exogenous. We do so because what a person chooses to do with the information that is carried in the experience may be different depending on its source.

An example may illustrate the point being made here. "Joyce" presents to treatment extremely upset. She is highly anxious that her boss is going to negatively judge the project that she and her colleague have been working on for two months. If it is Joyce's habitual pattern to be anxious about evaluations from others, if it is Joyce's habitual pattern that she regularly feels like she is not good enough, we may (as a heuristic) call this "Joyce's" self-as-bounded experience of anxiety. If, on the other hand, Joyce is typically a self-confident person who generally feels competent, we may wonder if there is something about her anxiety that is "not hers." Does her boss or the colleague with whom she is collaborating have feelings, needs, or fears that Joyce is experiencing as her own?

The ability to identify the source of her anxiety suggests a course of action to ameliorate it. If it is endogenous, or related to self-as-individual, it may be a question of self-soothing, or of self-talk that consists of Joyce reminding herself that this situation is not a repeat of past experiences. Perhaps the anxiety can best be managed by checking her feelings against the "evidence" in the here-and-now situation. You may explore with Joyce how the anxiety had value in past situations but is not appropriate to this one. How does the anxiety relate to her identity, self-esteem, and sense of agency? If it is one's "own," a number of different strategies may be effective in helping to metabolize the feeling. It may also point the way toward work that must be done on the self-as-individual level.

On the other hand, if this is not "Joyce's" anxiety, if this is her boss's, or maybe her colleague's, then the process of managing the feeling will be different. Simply noting "this is not mine" is often a very helpful strategy for clients who are not aware of the permeability of the self-boundary and the effects that others have on them. It may also generate additional strategies to manage the situation, such as finding ways to avoid contaiging the feeling or, when appropriate, addressing the other person's feelings as theirs or managing interactions with that person in a way that may minimize the contagion.

A related but slightly different situation has arisen repeatedly in this therapist's, supervisees', and consultees', practices. This is when a client presents with a high degree of anxiety/anger. After extensive exploration and attempts to help these clients regulate "their" anxiety, the situation does not improve. When the therapist shifts the focus away from "the client's" anxiety to ambient anxiety, the situation improves markedly. There is not a specific person from whom it emanates, or a single situation with which the anxiety is associated, but a collective anxiety that permeates the environment. When clients learn the degree to which their subjective experience of anxiety is the result of having a permeable boundary, the methods they can use to regulate differ from the ways they regulate more endogenous anxiety. They can engage in ongoing reflection of how/when/where they are soaking in ambient anxiety and make choices based on the source of the anxiety rather than on the subjective experience itself. The very notion of the anxiety being "not theirs" seems to have great value, bringing relief and a sense of greater balance and "sanity." As these examples make clear, understanding the permeability of the "self-boundary" is very important. Having a permeable self-boundary, understanding that some feelings one has are due to interactions with another person or the larger environment are not inherently pathological, but quite adaptive.

How do we help clients understand, value, and manage both the self-as-individual and the self-as-connected? The answer is that we help to teach them to use and appreciate their own intuition. Suggestions for how to do so are elaborated on in Chapter 7.

4.7 Practice Implications

One of the key quale that a mind-centered approach to therapy focuses on is the client's experience of what-it's-like to be "me." Ideally, this includes a sense of self that is both individual and separate as well as connected and permeable. In developing these dual aspects of the self, we help our clients work on the more traditional therapeutic aims of helping the clients enhance their self-esteem, agency, and personal responsibility. In fostering self-awareness, we help our clients identify when qualia are endogenous, or are auto-produced as part of their patterned way of being. We help our clients learn how to regulate effects that are associated with their self-as-individual.

We also help our clients recognize self-as-connected. We help them identify when qualia that they are experiencing may be the result of a contaiging affect from the environment (the endogenous mind). Ideally, our clients will learn how to use an endogenously generated information without suffering through holding on to it or mistaking it as their own. We also help them to recognize and take responsibility for the effect that they have on others. We help clients develop a sense of belonging to a larger entity, although we do not impose any sense of what, exactly, the nature of that entity may be. In doing so, our clients acquire a sense of belonging. They can celebrate their uniqueness, aware that what makes them unique is also an invaluable part of the connected whole to which they belong.

4.8 Conclusion

Without a high level of awareness of one's relatively stable pattern of perceiving and interpreting experience—an experience of the self as a separate, unique center of subjectivity—one may project their wishes, desires, and fears onto the world or, alternatively, feel like they have no agency. In either case, the failure to develop a sense of self as bounded may cause problems in living. At the other extreme, without an awareness of the permeability and connectedness of the self, one may think that they are personally responsible for feelings that they are not generating alone and have little ability to change. Alternatively, they may close off the capacity to apprehend a great deal of information from and about all that is beyond the ego. This limits the potential for one to respond appropriately, and equally causes problems in living. Thus, the ability to experience both the self-as-bounded and the self-as-permeable, and the ability to sense the difference between subjective experiences that are more endogenous versus those that are more exogenous, is healthy.

Relational Therapists have stressed the fact that a sense of self as a bounded individual with agency is crucial to mental well-being. They also have asserted that while this sense of self is fundamental to well-being, the development of this sense is in fact the result of the permeable nature of the boundary between self and other. The Relational Therapists bring their awareness of this permeability into the consulting room, allowing themselves to use it to better understand the internal experiences of their clients. Yet they do not suggest that it is equally important for clients to develop the sense of self-as-permeable to the degree that they develop the sense of individuality.

The Transpersonal Therapists have been clear that the sense of self-as-bounded ("reductive work," in the words of Scotton, 1985) is important to client well-being. They also stress that this is not sufficient for one to achieve the highest level of well-being. To do so, clients are helped to have a direct experience of the self as permeable and connected. In Transpersonal Therapy the level of connectedness is universal; the experience is of ontological oneness. Yet, it is possible that clients may also experience a better quality of life if they perceive the permeability of their self-boundary on a somewhat smaller scale. They may benefit from realizing the degree to which some of their subjective experiences are the result of interactions within the direct environment.

As Vaughan (1979a) so clearly illustrated, and as the participants in the author's research suggested, teaching clients to access and trust their intuition is an effective way to help them experience the differences between the two self-experiences. The participants in the research did not specify why or how this is so, but the work of Vaughan is instructive. The process of awakening to intuition is in fact the process of being able to apprehend both more endogenously generated and more exogenously generated subjective experiences and noting the difference between the two very similar phenomena. In this way, helping clients to develop their intuition helps them to have an experience of the self as both bounded and permeable. A subject to which we now turn.

4.9 Key Points

- As noted in Chapter 3, one may experience qualia that they produce routinely, based on past experiences and expectations, or one may experience qualia that they have contaged from the external environment.
- The sense of self as a bounded individual is associated with the ability to become aware of and take responsibility for qualia that are auto-generated. The sense of self as connected means that one is able to identify the external source of the qualia that they are experiencing.
- The sense of self as bounded means that we help clients work with self-awareness, identity, self-esteem, and agency.
- The sense of self as connected means that we help clients understand that they participate in a whole that is beyond their individuality.

4.10 References

Altman, N. (2020). Intersectionality: From politics to identity. In M. Belkin & C. White (Eds.), *Intersectionality and relational psychoanalysis: New perspectives on race, gender, and sexuality* (pp. 218–226). Routledge.

Aron, L. (1996). *A meeting of the minds: Mutuality in psychoanalysis.* The Analytic Press.

Beebe, B., Knoblauch, S., Rustin, J., & Sorter, D. (2005). *Forms of intersubjectivity in infant research and adult treatment.* Other Press.

Boston Change Process Study Group. (2010). *Change in psychotherapy: A unifying paradigm.* W. W. Norton.

Brown, R. S. (2017). *Psychoanalysis beyond the end of metaphysics: Thinking towards the post-relational.* Routledge.

Brown, R. S. (2020). *Groundwork for a transpersonal psychoanalysis: Spirituality, relationship, and participation.* Routledge.

Brown, O., Elkonin, D., & Naicker, S. (2013). The use of religion and spirituality in psychotherapy: Enables and barriers. *Journal of Religious Health, 52*, 1131–1146.

Crastnopol, M. (1995/2009). Anxiety. In M. Lionells, J. Fiscalini, C. H. Mann, & D. B. Stern (Eds.), *Handbook of interpersonal psychoanalysis* (pp. 139–164). Routledge. (Originally published in 1995 by The Analytic Press).

Ehrenberg, D. B. (1992). *The intimate edge.* W. W. Norton & Co.

Fonagy, P., Gergely, G., Jurist, E. L., & Target, M. (2002). *Affect regulation, mentalization, and the development of the self.* Other Press.

Jung, C. G. (1959/1978). Aion: Researches into the phenomenology of the self (R. F. C. Hull, Trans.). In H. Read et al. (Series Eds.), *The collected works of C. G. Jung* (Vol. 9, part 2). Princeton University Press.

Louchakova, O., & Lucas, M. K. (2007). Transpersonal self as a cultural category: Reflections on culture, and phenomenology. *Journal of Transpersonal Psychology, 39*(2), 111–136.

Mitchell, S. A. (1997). *Influence and autonomy in psychoanalysis.* The Analytic Press.

Rowan, J. (2002). A transpersonal way of relating to clients. *Journal of Contemporary Psychotherapy, 32*(1), 101–110.

Scotton, B. W. (1985). Observations on the teaching and supervision of transpersonal psychotherapy. *The Journal of Transpersonal Psychology, 17*(1), 57–75.

Stern, D. N. (1985). *The interpersonal world of the infant: A view from psychoanalysis and developmental psychology.* Basic Books.

Sullivan, H. S. (1954/1970). *The psychiatric interview: A guide for therapists and other interviewers, by the founder of the interpersonal theory of psychiatry.* W. W. Norton & Co.

Vaughan, F. (1979a). *Awakening intuition.* Anchor.

Vaughan, F. (1979b). Transpersonal psychotherapy: Context, content, and process. *The Journal of Transpersonal Psychology, 11*(2), 101–110.

Walsh, R., & Vaughan, F. (2018). Exploring consciousness: Fifty years of transpersonal studies. *The Journal of Transpersonal Psychology, 50*(1), 1–7.

Weigmann, K. (2013). Our sense of self. *European Molecular Biology Organization Reports, 14*(9), 765–768. https://doi.org/10.1038/embor.2013.124

Part II
The Practice of a Mind-Centered Depth Therapy (MCDT)

Intuition: Mind Knowing Mind   **5**

As important as theory and research are to the practice of therapy, these areas of knowledge are only valuable to the degree that they translate into doing. What do you do, how do you decide what to say next when a client who is in pain is sitting across from you, looking to you to help them?

The answer to the question, what do you do, may be misleading. You can't see mind working or changing. You may be able to observe that a therapist and client are "in sync," meaning that their body movements and vocal features are matched. For example, I may be nodding my head with the same intensity and at the same rate as my client is speaking. We may be moving our arms a similar distance from our bodies, in similar patterns. From the perspective of MCDT, all of the shared linguistic and paralinguistic features of our interaction are signs that something is going on inside and between us that cannot be witnessed. It is this internal experience that we are both having that is important. The way that I know what my client may be experiencing is through intuition. What I say or do next in the clinical encounter is based, to a very high degree, on intuition.

Intuition is at the heart of MCDT. But the definition of the term is not universally agreed upon. The definition one uses for the term depends on the perspective the person holds. In this chapter, we will look at different formulations of what, exactly, intuition might be. I include the analytic views; the business and cognitive psychology views; the psi views; and the instructions and experiences of intuitives, or psychics.

DOI: 10.4324/9781003090816-8

5.1 Psychoanalytic Views

The analytic views are complicated. In terms of the psychoanalytic thinkers, as my co-author and I discussed in *Intuition in Psychotherapy*, Freud himself seemed to either be ambivalent about the phenomenon or he changed his mind near the end of his career. He clearly denigrated intuition on a couple of occasions but expressed interest in telepathy a couple of times. This uncertainty seems to permeate psychoanalytic thought.

Piha (2005) wrote an extensive review of the various psychoanalytic attitudes toward intuition, which my co-author and I outlined in our book on clinical intuition. In his exposition, Piha (2005) recognizes a spectrum of orientations toward intuition. He shows that some analysts think that the belief that one is experiencing intuition involves pathological processes. Others are a bit less harsh and see it simply as an inferior way to process information. Those analysts who value intuition tend to see it as a form of unconscious communication between the client and therapist and they hold it to be an important tool in the clinical process. At the opposite end of the spectrum from those who pathologize intuition is the view that those who refuse to consider its value may be doing so due to pathological processes.

Not only did Freud express interest in telepathy, but he also highly valued unconscious communication. This is direct communication between the unconscious of the patient and the analyst. This theme was picked up and elaborated on by a number of his followers, so that the concept of unconscious communication is quite at home in psychoanalytic circles.

We see, then, that in psychoanalytic thought, there is a diversity of opinion on intuition, but there appears to be a nearly unanimous consent that there can be communication between two minds. As my co-author and I summarized in *Clinical Intuition*,

> The overwhelming point in the analytic literature of diverse schools is that two human minds are capable of interpenetrating and reciprocally influencing each other. One person can 'know' both some of the content as well as processes of another's mind without explicit verbal communication or deductive reasoning based on observable evidence.
>
> (Stickle & Arnd-Caddigan, 2019, p. 17)

This, as we will presently see, is precisely what I mean by the term "intuition."

5.2 Jung and the Post-Jungians

Jung and the post-Jungians, particularly the Transpersonal psychologists, also have important perspectives on intuition. Jung held a long-term interest in the occult, including mediumship. Indeed, his cousin was a medium and was the subject of Jung's doctoral dissertation. Goodheart's (1984) analysis of this work of Jung's suggests that the seances that produced the data for Jung's studies were saturated in implicit forms of interpersonal communication, or intuition. This suggests that Jung had personal experience with the phenomenon.

Pilard (2015) makes the point that Jung used the term "intuition" in a multitude of ways, and that the concept is "central and pivotal" in his work. Pilard explained that for Jung, intuition was the way to come to know the archetype God. She also discusses, in this context, Jung's treatment of empathy. In her exposition, she arrives at the conclusion that intuition joins the analyst and analysand: they "are one in empathy, in the shared created space of their under-conscious and the unconscious" (Pilard, 2015, p. 197). Pilard suggested that an important Jungian method to apply intuition to the project of uncovering the unconscious is active imagination. This technique will be explored in more detail in Chapter 7. From looking at Pilard's careful analysis of Jung's work, we arrive at the conclusion that from Jung forward there is agreement that there is an ability for individuals to share information via intuition.

Transpersonal psychology has significant Jungian influence. Among the early founders of Transpersonal psychology, Frances Vaughan (1979) wrote about methods for developing intuition and the value of doing so. She identified intuition as a means to access both personal memory and the collective or universal unconscious. It is clear that while Jung declared that the collective unconscious is psychological, as opposed to metaphysical, the Transpersonal psychologists do not follow suit. For Vaughan (1979), the universal unconscious is very much in keeping with the cosmopsychist ontology: the universal mind is the ground of all being. Intuition is the way to experience connection with the ground of all being in order to acquire information. In her work, it is clear that this includes information about and/or "from" another person.

5.3 Cognitive Theories

Business management and cognitive psychology researchers (I will combine them as "the cognitive theories") tend to be ensconced in academia, and they publish their research in traditional academic peer-reviewed journals. These researchers define intuition in a very particular way. They differentiate intuition from either insight or instinct and, instead, only call an experience intuition if it leads to a decision or judgment. That is, the individual decides on some action as a result of the experience. Their research tends to focus on questions that do not involve what another person is experiencing. Instead, the decisions in this research often center on facts about the physical world, and especially about the future (for example, whether or not one should buy a specific stock).

There are two different groups of theories that emanate from these researchers. One approach to intuition is called the heuristic model. Perhaps the most notable writer from this camp is Daniel Kahneman (2011). He has written a widely read book on the subject, and many people often are mistaken that his view is the "official" cognitive view of intuition. This is unfortunate because Kahneman has a fairly pessimistic assessment of the value of intuition, stressing the degree to which it is unreliable. The second group of theories take a more positive view of intuition. These theories center on learning models as the source of intuition.

These cognitive models, like William James and Jung before them, posit two different systems of thought:

> System 1 thinking and reasoning [intuition] is hypothesized as evolutionarily the more ancient of the two systems . . . its core processes are rapid, parallel, and automatic, permitting judgment in the absence of conscious reasoning. . . . System 2 deliberative problem solving is more recent, its core processes are slower, serial, and effortful, permitting conscious abstract reasoning and hypothetical thinking.
>
> (Gore & Sadler-Smith, 2011, p. 304)

Both models hold that intuition is the result of taking in information through the senses and processing it very quickly. The individual is not aware that they are taking in the information or that they are indeed processing it. It is this implicit activity that leads to a decision or a judgment. These researchers point to experts being able to make very fast decisions based on this process, such as a surgeon having a feeling that something is not right and then making a very fast decision to make an incision somewhere other than the site they had originally chosen.

5.4 Psi Research

There is another body of literature that is based on formal research called "psi" research. Psi is shorthand for psychic, and it centers on the activity of mind. Psi research is comprised of studies on paranormal phenomena. Because of their subject matter, much of this research is not conducted at universities but at free-standing institutes and foundations. The research tends to not be published in traditional academic peer-reviewed journals.

Perhaps among the more noted of these researchers, Dean Radin (1997, 2006) has long held a view consistent with cosmopsychism: the world has a global mind, or there is a "non-local intelligence permeating space and time" (1997, p. 173), and there is a fundamental connection between everything in the universe. Indeed, he states, "our brains and minds are in intimate communion with the universe. It's as though we lived in a gigantic bowl of clear jello. Every wiggle—every movement, event, and thought—within that medium is felt throughout the entire bowl" (2006, p. 263). He clarifies that the jello metaphor is imprecise to the degree that the medium is not material, as jello may suggest. Intuition, from this view, is the effect of one instance of the universal mind (an individual) connecting and sharing information with another instance of the universal mind. This is consistent with the cosmopsychist view of mind.

5.5 Intuitives

Yet another group of writers that have important insights into intuition are people who use their intuition to earn a living. These people are sometimes called psychics or intuitives. The books that they write are written on the popular level. Their work is not based on formal research, although many of these authors have studied the subject for many years. The strength of these books is that the people who write them are able to talk about what works for them and what does not work for them. In many of these books, we see a definition of intuition that is some form of "knowing without knowing how you know." These writers, in particular, have a great deal of insight into how to develop your intuition, which is the subject of the next chapter.

5.6 A Mind-Centered Definition of Intuition

Keeping these sources in mind, I have arrived at a definition of intuition that I use in MCDT that is consistent with a cosmopsychist worldview. Recall that in Chapter 1 I discussed intuition as an epistemological tool. In plain English that means that intuition is a way to know about reality. It is knowledge specifically about the mind aspect of the universe.

In the Stickle and Arnd-Caddigan (2019) study, the participants stated that the way they "had" an intuition was through purely subjective experiences, such as mental images and sounds, sensations, and emotions. These experiences cannot be detected by an external observer. And, like all mental phenomena, they cannot be measured. They exist as qualities, rather than being quantifiable. In other words, intuition is experienced as qualia, or mind. We use mind to know mind. This is what intuition is: knowing mind by means of mind. Put another way, it is the experience of the transfer of information between individual instances of mind.

Okay, but how do you *do* that?! There are a few parts to the answer to that question. Again, you must be clear that the process is mental. It is more a question of what it will be like for you and your client to be in this kind of interaction. This is about subjective experiences that you will both have.

We must immediately note that the knowledge you attain in this way is not completely accurate, and you must engage in a continual process of checking and verifying this knowledge. This will be addressed in Chapter 7. As discussed in Chapter 2, your mind and your client's mind become more coherent, complex, and flexible in the process of being connected to another mind. Thus, the use of intuition not only helps you know about the client, and thus help you to guide the therapeutic process in a productive direction, but also it is a process that is, in and of itself, mutative.

5.7 Conclusion

This very brief review of the ways that various thinkers have defined intuition forms the basis for a definition of the term that I use in MCDT. Psychoanalysts and Analytical psychologists agree that therapists and clients share mental contents and processes in the course of treatment, and that this process is essential in therapy. The Transpersonal psychologists and the psi literature add that this activity can be understood if we hold an ontological position akin to that of cosmopsychism: mind is singular and universal, thus individual instances of mindedness have a shared ground. From the Cognitive theorists, we accept the proposition that intuition is a form of mental activity that is not discursive or linear, but is instant and global knowing, which intuitives describe as knowing without knowing how you know.

These descriptions coalesce to arrive at the mind-centered definition of the term. This is that intuition is a subjective, qualitative experience that is the result of a mind acquiring information from a mind.

Using intuition in therapy requires that you have developed your general intuition to a fairly high degree. Some of you may be using your intuition in your daily life quite comfortably. For those of you who are less inclined to do so, there are several things you can do to improve this natural capacity, to which we will turn in the next chapter.

5.8 Key Point

The definition of intuition used in this book is that it is the ability for an instance of mind to acquire information directly from another instance of mind.

5.9 References

Goodheart, W. G. (1984). C. G. Jung's first "patient": On the seminal emergence of Jung's thought. *Journal of Analytical Psychology, 29,* 1–34.

Gore, J., & Sadler-Smith, E. (2011). Unpacking intuition: A process and outcome framework. *Review of General Psychology, 15,* 304–316.

Kahneman, D. (2011). *Thinking, fast and slow.* Farrar, Strauss, and Giroux.

Piha, H. (2005). Intuition: A bridge to the coenesthetic world of experience. *Journal of the American Psychoanalytic Association, 53*(1), 23–49.

Pilard, N. (2015). *Jung and intuition: On the centrality and variety of forms of intuition in Jung and post-Jungians.* Karnac.

Radin, D. (1997). *The conscious universe: The scientific truth of psychic phenomena.* Harper One.

Radin, D. (2006). *Entangled minds: Extrasensory experiences in a quantum reality.* Paraview Pocket Books.

Stickle, M., & Arnd-Caddigan, M. (2019). *Clinical intuition: From research to practice.* Routledge.

Vaughan, F. (1979). *Awakening intuition.* Anchor.

Developing General Intuition 6

Once you have decided that intuition may be a valuable tool in your clinical practice, there are several practices you can engage in to help you develop it. To do so requires a good deal of preparatory work. If you have made the decision to become more intuitive, you may want to prepare both your body and your mind to understand and use intuitively derived information. I discuss mindfulness practices—meditation and centering prayer—at length in this context because mindfulness is perhaps the most robust method to prepare your mind to register intuitive knowledge. As well as preparing your body and mind, highly intuitive people have noted that certain character traits and engaging in creative pursuits are helpful in promoting intuition.

After you have prepared, practicing the ability to "catch" intuitions will help you become more adept. You will want to know what to look for. But because projection and true intuition feel so much alike, you may want to track your experiences. By doing so, you can start to see differences between what these two experiences feel like. Finally, you may want to join with others who can support you, and perhaps provide some guidance, as you develop your intuition.

6.1 Developing Intuition

I am using the term "general intuition" to refer to intuition in everyday, non-clinical circumstances. There is a good bit of literature on how to develop general intuition. Some of the accounts are very spiritually

DOI: 10.4324/9781003090816-9

oriented and may not be appropriate for people who do not endorse a spiritual orientation. Other books on developing intuition are written from the cognitive psychology/business management perspective. This orientation requires that the word "intuition" be limited to decision-making circumstances. Perhaps the largest group of books on developing intuition comes from writers who use their intuition professionally. In reviewing a number of such texts, there arise clear commonalities. As a qualitative researcher, I see great value in noting the areas of agreement (see Appendix A for a list of the books I consulted, along with the authors' recommendations for developing intuition).

6.2 Preparatory or Indirect Practices

Like any ability you wish to enhance, regular practice is important. This includes repeating activities that will prepare you to enhance your intuition but are not the direct accessing of intuitively derived information. As an analogy, when I began taking individual yoga lessons, my instructor suggested that I engage in some strength training in the form of working out with dumbbells. While lifting the weights is not yoga, it sure did improve my ability to practice yoga. These preparatory practices will likewise help you improve your intuition.

6.2.1 Extend an Invitation

A few of the recommendations for developing intuition suggest that you begin from a position of valuing intuition, recognizing its legitimacy and merit, and then set an intention to enhance your own intuitive capacity. Beginning from a place of doubt and/or the expectation that you will not gain any valuable information from your intuition, or fear that you may be doing something "wrong" or "bad" by pursing enhanced intuitive capacity, is a recipe for failure. Intuition is the activity of your mind, and therefore your mindset is foundational.

I would like to suggest that the directive to "set an intention" may be misleading to some. If, by that phrase, you are imagining exerting your will in order to become more intuitive, then the suggestion will not be helpful. Instead, the experience is more akin to offering an invitation. It is a softening of your self-boundary to allow what comes. It is a receptive state.

6.2.2 Self-Care

Part of the ancillary practice of intuition is self-care. Sleep, healthy food, exercise, and a stable mindset-set the stage to make the most of your intuitive ability. Your mind and body must be healthy so that you can reach beyond your immediate needs.

6.2.3 Body Work: Exercise and Relaxation

You may wish to engage in preparatory work with your mind and your body (remember, they are part of a single whole). Body work that may enhance intuition can include regular exercise. The participants in my previous research suggested that rhythmic, repetitive forms of cardio exercise are helpful, such as running, walking, swimming, etc. Yoga has been noted repeatedly as helpful in enhancing intuitive abilities—in the books on intuition I analyzed as well as by the participants in my research on clinical intuition. This makes sense: if your body is in pain, if you are physically fatigued, etc., it will be very difficult for you to focus on any other qualia. Therefore, taking care of your body so that you can access other, more subtle experiences of what-it's-like to be you will be important.

Regular practices in which you relax your body are also important. In the big world of de-stress literature and videos, you can easily access a variety of ways of inducing relaxation. A common such exercise is progressive relaxation. In this exercise, you can lay down comfortably and imagine relaxing parts of your body in succession. You can start from the bottom and go up or from the top and go down your body. So, for example, you may focus on your feet, drawing your awareness to how they feel, then instructing yourself to relax your feet. Perhaps you want to wiggle your toes a bit to help you let go of tension. Spend as much time relaxing your feet as you need. Then move up to your ankles, calves, knees, thighs, hips, lower abdomen, lower back, mid-section, chest, upper back, shoulders, down the top of the arms, elbows, lower arms, hands, fingers, neck, back of your head, face, and top of your head. I cue myself with images, such as imagining a tight muscle as a block of ice cream, melting, softening, dripping. Or a knot in a rope that gradually loosens and opens. A very powerful relaxation exercise is Yoga Nidra. Yoga Nidra goes beyond physical relaxation and is a powerful meditative exercise as well.

6.2.4 Preparatory Mental Work: Self-Work

Besides the preparatory physical work, there is likewise preparatory mental work. This may include a number of processes. Perhaps the most central aspect of our mental functioning is our sense of self. Self-work is foundational to accurate intuition. What are your patterns? These are your routine ways of perceiving and interpreting experience. These are the expectations you bring into the world based on what you have experienced in the past. They also include your needs, desires, wishes, motivations, and fears. Ultimately, the biggest barrier to intuition is projecting these onto the world. In some cases, what feels like intuition may be wish-fulfillment; in other cases, it may be seeing yourself in others. Thus, you must have, to the degree that any of us has, an ability to spot the possibility that you are projecting your perceptions or needs onto a situation rather than receiving new awareness of what is.

I must emphasize that nobody is completely able to identify all of their habitual patterns. There is no such thing as complete self-awareness. This is like looking under the rug on which you are standing. If you know that you don't know what the bottom of the rug actually looks like, but that it is different from the top of the rug, and you are able to look at some of the corners, you are doing the most that one can do. This means that the effort is important, and never-ending.

It is also important to remember that all subjective experiences feel like they are happening to "me," so it is difficult to determine the difference between those we automatically generate from our patterned way of being and those that are the result of taking in qualia from an outside source. As intuition is ultimately the information we are able to take in from beyond ourselves, we must be able to differentiate between what we are applying to a situation and what we are receiving from the situation.

Self-work also includes the ability to bring awareness to qualia as they arise. To register intuitive information, you must be able to "catch" subtle subjective experiences that are fleeting, as well as regulate the profoundly impactful qualia. You must be able to tune into rising images, internal sounds, sensations, emotions, tastes, smells, or any other subjective experience that crosses your mind. These are the forms that intuition take; this is how the information registers to you. Learning to "catch" the passing experiences, and to regulate the more overwhelming ones, will help you perceive and use the information your intuition offers.

All of these aspects of mental work can be achieved through the practice of mindfulness. Intuition is opening or extending your mind to connect with mind beyond you. This requires a deep familiarity with mind and a sense of connectedness to that which is beyond your limited mind. For this reason, regular mindfulness practice (meditation, centering prayer, or some other form) is central to building your ease and accuracy with intuition. You may be very aware of mindfulness practices, as they have been incorporated into a number of approaches to therapy, including psychodynamic and cognitive-behavioral. Two mindfulness practices that have been researched in the psychotherapy and counseling literature are various forms of meditation and centering prayer.

Meditation practice can help you achieve many of the other qualities that are associated with intuition, such as relaxation, self-awareness, and a non-judgmental stance toward experience. Over time, regular meditation brings an attitude of acceptance, which is associated with enhancing intuition. A related capacity associated with meditation is non-attachment, which is accepting what is rather than trying to force what you want. To repeat, forcing your desires or fears onto the world is one of the chief barriers to accurate intuition.

Meditation is self-monitoring, or watching the mind and the body. As you do this, you become aware of processes, both mental and physical. You can recognize what is happening in the present moment without judging it, either via attachment or aversion. One of the reasons meditation is so helpful to the development of intuition is that in noting what arises, you will see patterns. This will help you be able to determine. as you experience qualia. which are "yours" and which qualia are about something or someone outside of you.

There are different "types" of meditation or approaches to the practice. These are in fact techniques; technique is not meditation. All techniques lead to a common state, which is to stop your typical mental processes in order to experience the relationship between your mind and the universal mind. Fortunately, this realization is not required in order for meditation to help you become more intuitive. Meditation techniques include focusing your attention on various experiences. Among these are:

- Your breath.
- Your mental processes.
- Your body / movement.
- A sound or image in your imagination.
- An imaginary process (creative visualization).
- A sound or object outside of you (the sound of a gong; a candle flame, etc.).
- An abstract concept (like impermanence).
- You can engender a specific emotion (like compassion).
- There are forms of Zen meditation where the meditator continually engages in processes to make their mind blank (like imagining thoughts projected onto a white wall, and sweeping them away, or thoughts being enclosed in a bubble and floating away).
- A divinity.

How do you meditate? The simple answer is this: every "rule" for what you "have to" do to meditate or how you "should" meditate is a potential excuse to not meditate.

- Meditate at a time that works, for a period of time that works. Start small, like 5 or 10 minutes. You can build up to longer periods of time.
- Practice in a place that is relatively free of distractions. What focuses one person may be a terrible distraction for another. For example, I hate bells and chanting going on while I'm trying to meditate. Some people find them really helpful. Some people find music distracting, some find it helpful. Find what works for you.
- Be comfortable. You want to wear clothes that will not bind or pinch. Sit in a posture that you can hold for a sustained period of time. This may start out as supported, in a chair or with some pillows. Close your eyes or simply lower your gaze to the floor. Your eyelids and focus should be relaxed.
- Once you've established a habitual practice, then you can experiment with different postures, times, circumstances, methods, etc.

So many experienced meditators have shared their wisdom about what has and has not worked for them and their students. All of this wisdom is wonderful, but if there are so many different experiences of what works, then obviously what works for one will not work for all. Take guidance, but do not be fooled by orthopraxy (the need to do what you're told). Anyone who tries to tell you that you MUST meditate one way or another may be having difficulty understanding that people are different.

As you meditate, there are several different experiences you may have. Some of them may feel like "I'm not doing this right. . . . this isn't working." But that's not accurate. If you notice that your mind is active, and you can notice what it is doing, that's exactly what's supposed to happen! Some common experiences include (but are not limited to):

- Emotions.
- Physical sensations.
- Memories.
- Images.
- Energetic sensations.
- Fantasies (what might happen in your future, or some kind of daydream, realistic or not). This might include rehearsing a conversation that you think you may or may not have with someone.

- Thinking: This can include:
  - What you need to do or should do or haven't yet done.
  - How you can describe what you experienced when you meditated.
  - You can think about a problem that you need to solve.
- Insight: You might achieve some profound understanding about:
  - Yourself.
  - Your interpersonal dynamics.
  - Another person.
  - The nature of the universe.

Some of these are really cool. Some are frustrating. All of them are simply to be noted with interest. None of them mean you have failed, and none of them mean you are enlightened. It's all just part of the process.

I have taught a number of Christian students who are uncomfortable with meditation. Some have been taught that the practice is dangerous or goes against their religion. If your faith tradition teaches any objections to meditation, you may wish to pursue an alternative mindfulness approach: centering prayer. While centering prayer was developed by Christians, it can be adjusted to fit other religious orientations that support a belief in a deity or deities.

Centering prayer is an awareness practice that is a synthesis of various sources from the Christian contemplative tradition. It is the seeking of a distinctive connection or bond with God, in which you abandon your own agenda. It is based on the belief that the divine presence is available to everyone at every moment, but one's worldview typically blocks this awareness. Centering prayer is thus seen as an opportunity to "wake up" to this divine presence. You don't have to do anything to get it, you are already there. This is how P. Gregg Blanton (2011) describes the practice:

1. Choose a sacred word—any word that elicits a sense of the love of God— as a symbol of your intention to consent to God's presence and action within. The focus is not on the word but on the indwelling of God. You simply use the word to bring you back to the real focus—the indwelling. If you can't find a word that works for you, you can choose to focus on a sound or your breathing as a symbol for the "spirit."
2. Sit quietly and comfortably with your eyes closed, and silently bring the word to your mind as a symbol for your consent to God's presence and action within you. You are opening to God and putting yourself at God's disposal. This is a surrendering to God's action. The stress in centering

prayer is on receptivity to God as a way of unloading deep rooted, unconscious tensions (Ferguson et al., 2009).
3. When you become aware that thoughts are arising, you silently remind yourself of the sacred word. There are 4 R's in centering prayer: Resist no thought, Retain no thought, React to no thought, and Return to the sacred word. The sacred word is used to release, not repress, thoughts.
4. When you are done, remain silent with your eyes closed for a couple of minutes to transition back to daily life. Carry the attitude of attention to God throughout your daily life.

Notice that this activity is opening. As we will see in the next chapter, opening to the mind of another (or extending your mind) is a central feature of clinical intuition.

Mindfulness practices are a good way to mentally prepare for intuition. These practices help you tune into the qualia that you need to be able to "catch" in order to gain knowledge or insight, and provide an enhanced understanding of your endogenous experiences. They help provide the mental stability necessary to use intuition most productively.

6.2.5 Character

Another important area of your life that is related to enhanced intuition is your values or morality. The literature on intuition often stresses a number of character traits that are important for its development. It would seem that having certain virtues or characteristics can help one become more intuitive. Among these are humility, honesty, kindness, understanding, and optimism. Characterological barriers to intuition include selfishness, self-delusion, ego, arrogance, fear of failure, and self-imposed limitations that arise from social conditioning and belief systems. This self-work and self-awareness is often most easily accomplished through your own personal insight-oriented therapy.

6.2.6 Creativity

Intuitive people often engage in creative and non-verbal forms of expression. This may be helpful in refining intuition because intuition has often been associated with the kind of thinking that is also associated with creativity. William James, Carl Jung, and cognitive scientists who have studied intuition have all suggested that we can think in a linear, directed, logical, verbal manner, or we can think in an associative, non-verbal manner that is associated with reverie, daydreaming, and intuition. Your intuition may improve the more comfortable you become with this second form of thinking. Engaging in creative activities may be helpful in doing so. Allowing yourself time to daydream may also serve this purpose. In any event, letting go of the logical, rational, problem-solving mode of thinking is necessary to enhance intuition.

Develop Your Intuition

Prepare

> Extend an invitation for intuitive insights.
> Self-work.
> Take care of your body.
> Know your mental patterns.
> Practice mindfulness.
> Develop your character.
> Engage in creative practices.

Direct Practices

> Be open to receive.
> Clarify the information you are seeking.
> You may choose to use an aid, such as tarot cards, a candle flame, a bowl of water, etc.
> Identify subtle, passing forms of intuition.
> Write down your experience and the meaning you attach to it.
> Over time, discern which experiences are validated and which are not.
> Enlist support; work with others who value intuition.

6.3 Direct Practice

Laying the groundwork for intuition is important. Once you have built the metaphorical muscles, you are ready to directly access your intuition. Practicing intuition in the moment means opening to and "catching" often fleeting experiences. The first step is to open yourself. This can be done by actively symbolizing the process of opening (like visualizing, or somatically feeling, a process of opening), or by passively ceasing effort and allowing qualia to arise. The next step is to catch the qualia that arise. In the past, you may have dismissed these experiences as distractions and worked to re-orient your attention to the task at hand. You may have ignored them, or perhaps did not even register them. Intuition requires that you tune in to passing qualia.

The qualia can take many forms. They may be mental images or actual visual distortions in how you perceive something in your environment. For example, in my research on clinical intuition, one participant talked about features of people's bodies seeming to get bigger or smaller. Another participant talked about everything but one point of focus becoming fuzzy. It may take an auditory form: you may hear "in your head" sounds, words, or snippets of poems or song lyrics. It may be that when you hear something from your environment (someone else speaking to you or someone else, something on the radio, etc.), a word or phrase seems "hot," or is somehow emphasized. Intuition may come as a physical feeling. A "gut feeling" is one of the more common forms, but people have related feeling their chests, heads, the skin on their arms, and a host of other physical sensations. Some people have reported smelling specific things as a form of intuition. Again, in my research, one person discussed family members who smelled grass or roses when someone close had recently passed away. Sometimes it feels like you suddenly just know something. You may experience the onset of an emotion, again, often seemingly out of nowhere. Some people have reported that they feel energy: the flow of energy, or sudden changes in energy. Your job is to pay attention to these subtle experiences and begin to learn which ones are associated with useful information.

You may choose to engage in more formal "sessions" to access your intuition. This may take a form that is very similar to a mindfulness practice. Sit comfortably, quiet your mind and body, and simply attend to whatever arises. Open yourself to receive information that will be helpful to yourself or another person. It may be helpful to imagine opening in some way. You may visualize a flower blooming, or a dot expanding and becoming nebulous. Perhaps you have a specific question, or perhaps you simply have a general desire for a helpful insight. Be clear regarding what you are asking for. At the end of the practice, you may wish to write down what you experienced and how you interpret that experience. This will be discussed more in a moment as journal writing. You may choose to use some form of cuing tool, such as tarot or oracle cards, or to look into a bowl of water, a candle flame, etc. If you use cards, I highly recommend that you do not look at an interpretation of the card but look at the card and note what arises within you.

6.3.1 Journaling

Another part of the regular practice to improve intuition is journal keeping. Record experiences that seem intuitive. Note the details of what you experienced and the situational context in which they arose, as well as the information that came to you. It is important to record when they turn out to be accurate. This will help you begin to discern the differences between those experiences that reflect true intuition and those that are the result of you sensing the situation through the filter of your own patterns, needs, wishes, etc. Another good reason to write down your experiences is that it may not be immediately obvious what the experience means. I know of a person who had a vivid vision that kept coming up for her. She had no idea what it meant until years later. Then the pandemic arrived. Because of the vision, she knew at the first report of a pandemic that it would be associated with major upheaval. She was both psychologically and materially prepared for the quarantine and subsequent social unrest.

6.3.2 Enlist Support

Joining a support group—or finding a supportive friend or mentor—may help with a number of the recommendations for developing intuition. It may help you develop greater trust, openness, honesty, and the ability to discern your patterns of projecting. It may spur you to engage in regular practices and support you in building the associated character traits. It may also help you feel that you are not becoming psychologically unsound as you begin to shift your understanding of the nature of the universe and the possibility of "paranormal" abilities. If you can find someone to work with who has greater experience in using their intuition, you may benefit from the same process that is beneficial in MCDT; the creation of a shared mind-space may help you open your mind to become more flexible, complex, and coherent. This will help you as you move forward on the path of accessing intuitive information.

Psychotherapy and counseling require a high level of professionalism. Given that intuition is still considered "woo-woo" and some kind of alternative to professional practice, it is incumbent on you to make sure that you are using intuition appropriately. We will look at the clinical applications of intuition in the next chapter. In this chapter, I hope to emphasize that in order to apply your intuition in the consulting room, you must be comfortable with it in your life. The tips in this chapter will help you build your capacity to access your intuition before you bring it to your clinical practice.

6.4 Conclusion

Much of the focus of this chapter on developing intuition was on engaging in a mindfulness practice. Two such practices are meditation and centering prayer. I have stressed these practices in a chapter on developing intuition because intuition requires that you open or extend your mind as well as know the difference between your mind and the mind beyond you. These practices are particularly well suited to these ends.

Meditation and centering prayer are part of the preparatory work we must do to hone our intuition. Preparatory work includes self-care, such as proper sleep, nutrition, and so forth. A healthy body includes exercise. People who are highly intuitive suggest that rhythmic movement is especially helpful, as is the practice of yoga.

Intuition also requires a great deal of mental preparation. This includes self-work; knowing your patterns and typical ways of experiencing are very important. It also includes the ability to register very subtle qualia as they arise. The ability to note internal experiences, as well as apparent distortions in the external environment, is fundamental to intuition. Again, mindfulness practices are also very important to the mental preparation for intuition. Meditation, centering prayer, or other such practices help you become familiar with your mind and open or extend it.

People who are highly intuitive have noted that developing your character is important in developing intuition. There are certain attributes that seem to invite intuitive ability. Creative activity has also been repeatedly noted as helpful in developing intuition. It may be that this practice helps us tap into "system 1" or associative, non-linear thought that is key to intuition.

The direct practice of intuition can include regular periods of inviting intuitive insights. You might want to use props to help you, or not. Journaling is an important part of this process, as it provides necessary feedback for which circumstances are associated with which experiences that provide accurate intuitive insights. Finally, joining a support group or finding a friend or mentor is recommended in developing your intuition. Once you are comfortable with your intuition, you can take the next step and begin to introduce this capacity into the consulting room.

6.5 Key Points

- Intuition is knowing without knowing how you know; it is the acquisition of information through connection with mind beyond our individual mind.
- Developing your general intuition is necessary before you introduce it into the clinical context.
- To develop your general intuition, you can engage in a number of practices.

These include preparatory practices as well as practicing the use of your intuition in more direct ways.

- One preparatory practice that may be the most important in developing intuition is mindfulness. You may engage in a number of techniques to meditate, or engage in centering prayer.

- The direct practice of accessing intuition requires that you tune into a number of different forms of qualia. These may seem very subtle. Catching them is key. They may come to you during a formal practice, or they come suddenly, without warning.

- The direct practice of intuition requires that you document your experiences, in order to begin to discern which experiences are helpful, and which experiences do not supply useful information, but are projections of your wishes, needs, habitual patterns, etc.

- Joining with others who value and use intuition is very helpful. Finding a group, a friend, or a mentor will help you as you find your worldview changing.

6.6 References

Blanton, P. G. (2011). The other mindful practice: Centering prayer & psychotherapy. *Pastoral Psychology, 60*, 133–147.

Ferguson, J. K., Willemsen, E. W., & Castaneto, M. V. (2009). Centering prayer as a healing response to everyday stress: A psychological and spiritual process. *Pastoral Psychology, 59*, 305–329.

Using Intuition in Therapy: Clinical Intuition and Intuitive Inquiry

7

In the last chapter, we reviewed some practices that can help you develop your intuition. These practices are foundational to using intuition in the clinical context. There are also additional exercises and conditions that are important to this endeavor. You may want to engage in some methods between sessions to help you with your clinical intuition. There are also techniques that you might employ during sessions in order to enhance your ability to gain important information about your client and the therapeutic process.

It must be immediately noted that if you are going to use intuition to help in your professional practice, you must keep in the forefront of your mind the fact that the clinical application of this capacity is a special context. As a licensed professional psychotherapist or counselor, you have a fiduciary responsibility to your client. You must act with the client's best interests, well-being, autonomy, and self-determination at the center of everything you do. This places some special conditions on using your intuition as the center-piece of the healing relationship.

The major "technique" in MCDT is intuitive inquiry. Based on the Relational Analytic Methods of detailed inquiry, sustained empathic inquiry, and sustained empathic immersion, intuitive inquiry targets all three of the muta-tive aspects of treatment: it helps the client become more aware of—and thus able to better regulate—their mental patterns; it contributes to a new kind of relationship; and it creates a mental connection that helps the client gain more mental flexibility, complexity, and coherence.

DOI: 10.4324/9781003090816-10

7.1 Clinical Intuition

Using clinical intuition can be conceptualized as having two aspects: intersession practices and in-session practices. Many of these methods are the same as those in which you may engage to enhance your general intuition. In addition, there are specific things you must do to apply intuition to the clinical context in order to support therapeutic goals and the client's best interests.

It must be stressed again that intuition, or what feels like intuition, can be wrong. Given the clinical imperative to work for the client's best interests, this means that the therapist who uses intuition must be very careful in its application. What leads people astray in terms of judging the accuracy of an intuitive sense is when one mistakes their own patterns of perceiving and interpreting, or endogenous material, for information about or coming from their client (exogenous material). My own research (Stickle & Arnd-Caddigan, 2019) and that of Witteman et al. (2012) found that projection, countertransference, and confirmation bias are major factors that undermine the accuracy of intuition. As we have noted in relation to general intuition, self-awareness is the antidote. Beyond mere awareness, however, a therapist must be able to regulate their own needs, desires, and expectations in order to use intuition professionally. I have suggested elsewhere (Arnd-Caddigan, 2019) that this means that engaging in education/training, supervision, and consultation with other therapists who use intuition professionally can help to bring this level of self-awareness and self-control to the therapist who wishes to use intuition clinically.

Intuition has been judged by some people to be the opposite of discursive, logical thought. Yet some of the participants in my previous study noted that they saw discursive thought and intuition as equally useful and, in fact, intertwined. To that end, they indicated that their clinical intuition was enhanced by engaging in more standard preparatory behaviors. For example, they stated that they reviewed whatever documentation might be available, including records, reports, and/or assessments.

The intuitive therapists in the study also discussed the need to be able to apply formal theory in combination with intuition. Training, including continuing education that focuses on theory, is imperative. Taken together, the use of records and theory indicate that intuitive therapists are able to integrate discursive, logical thought processes with the more associative and holistic thought that is associated with intuition. This appears to be an important ability to develop in order to maximize the utility of clinical intuition.

Another extra-therapeutic activity that can help you use your intuition ethically and appropriately is to seek consultation. This can be in the form of a small peer-group of therapists with whom you can discuss your cases, focusing on experiences with clinical intuition. This must include honesty about when intuition was helpful, and when it was not, as well as openness to feedback concerning your own patterns that you may be imposing on your professional work. Likewise, you may choose to work with a mentor or consultant regarding your use of clinical intuition.

There is one specific exercise in which I engage between sessions in order to utilize intuitive insights concerning the treatment. Several years ago, I noted that I used this tool and undertook research to see if other therapists used it as well. What I do is have "imaginary conversations" with my clients. I published two articles about the findings of my study. Indeed, therapists of diverse theoretical orientations reported having imaginary conversations with their clients, and found that they were able to gain important information. At the time I wrote the results of the study, I attributed the knowledge to neurochemical processes. If I were to replicate the study today, I would interpret the findings as evidence for the usefulness of this technique for accessing intuition. Perhaps the most interesting aspect of the exercise for me today is the degree to which it is clearly Jungian, being quite consistent with his method of active imagination. As we will see in the next chapter, Jung held that imagination, and especially the technique of active imagination, is an important way to access intuition.

When I decided to research imaginary conversations with a client, it was in response to me noticing that I was engaging in such a conversation, and that in fact this is something I do regularly. I was gardening, and completely absorbed, completely unaware of what I was doing mentally. When I pulled back and reflected on my mental activity, I began to analyze it. I was picturing my client in my mind. He was sitting in my office in his usual place. Just as in actual sessions, in my imagination I "saw" his facial expression and his movements. I could hear the tone and volume and rate of his speech. I heard "his" voice. I asked him the question that had clinically eluded me: why are you so defended against the idea that other people are different and separate from you? Why is it so important for you to try to control others? He "answered" my question! I was able to meet him in his next session with the provisional insight into the dynamics involved in his struggle with his girlfriend. As we will see in a bit, I slowly introduced some of the insights I gained during my imaginary conversation, which step by step helped him reflect on the motivations, needs, and desires that he had previously not been able to grasp.

There are also a host of things you can do during a session to enhance your clinical intuition. The first is to establish a connection with your client. The therapists in the Petitmengin-Peugeot (1999) study stated that the way they cultivate a feeling of connection with their clients is by focusing on specific sites of their bodies while they generate visual, kinesthetic, and/or auditory images of connections. These can take any number of forms, such as a channel of light or energy vibration that creates a bridge between the therapist and the client. Charles (2004) also studied therapists who used their intuition professionally, and they supported the Petitmengin-Peugeot findings. The therapists described the degree to which their whole bodies were implicated in this sense of connectedness with their clients. I personally center on a desire to see the world through my client's eyes. I'm not sure why "eyes" are important, but I try to literally see the world through their eyes.

Clinical intuition also requires that you cultivate a sense of openness and receptivity in the actual session itself. This exercise was explored in the previous chapter in terms of developing your general intuition. Research (Charles, 2004) suggests that opening and preparing yourself to receive just before or during a session with a client can be helpful. This is referenced in the therapy literature in several ways. Freud (1912) called it "evenly hovering attention." Bion (1965/2015) referenced being with your client "without memory or desire." Geller and Greenburg (2012) have written about "therapeutic presence." All of these phrases point to an attitude of acceptance of what is. This means that you are not trying to "get" your client to come to any particular insight or conclusion or understanding. It means that you bracket whatever you think is best for your client. It means that you do not know what or how they "should" be thinking or behaving or feeling, and you are not invested in finding the solution to their problem. Instead, you are entering the stream of their experience, even while you keep one foot on the shoreline of your professional perspective to avoid being swept into the rapids.

To avoid being swept away, you must be grounded and centered in the face of your client's sometimes overwhelming experience. Again, while engaging in grounding exercises can be very helpful in general, doing so in the moment in session is an important capacity in order to receive clear intuitive information in a storm of feelings. There is a host of grounding exercises available on the internet. Examples of such exercises include exhaling mindfully, then focusing on the contact points between yourself and the ground or your chair, feeling gravity's pull on your body. Another grounding practice may be to visualize a chord from deep in the earth through your body. Likewise, centering exercises are readily available on the internet. Among these you might focus on your solar plexus or your chest/heart. Both grounding and centering are ways to keep yourself connected to your own experience in the present moment so that you don't become overwhelmed by exogenous subjectivity, or those experiences that you are purposefully contaiging from your client in order to know about your client's mental processes and contents.

The next step is to tune in to yourself. In doing so, you train your awareness on the subtle qualia that signal the influx of intuitive information. Based on my prior research, you may wish to attend to what you feel, both emotionally and somatically. Notice what you hear "in your head": tones or words or lyrics, as well as sounds from outside of yourself that stand out. This can mean something that sounds particularly loud, or heavily stressed, or "off," etc. There may be symbols or associations that arise, or in some cases just a sense of knowing that can wash over you. You may note a pull to say or do something that feels like it is independent of your agency (with care in acknowledging any proclivity you may have for impulsiveness). The different subjective experiences you can have are almost limitless. The point is, note all passing qualia. If mind can be shared, and can only be known through subjective experience, the acquisition of information gained through a shared mental state with your client will always take the form of a subjective experience.

You must also center on your client. This can include all of their paralinguistic behavior, but more deeply it means centering yourself on what it is like to be who they are and what it is like *for them* to have had their unique personal experiences. Many of the respondents in the Stickle and Arnd-Caddigan (2019) study suggested that centering on your client has two benefits. First, the paralinguistic communication—vocal qualities, like tone of voice, vocal prosody, rate, pitch, etc. as well as body language, like gestures, muscle tension, facial expressions, etc.—is a form of direct communication. But, equally, they suggest that focusing this closely on your client in-and-of-itself enhances intuition.

The participants in my previous research also disclosed that they had a third focal point. This is the context or the connection between the therapist and the client. This is the therapeutic field. It is a place in-between the therapist and the client, or the medium in which their minds meet.

Once you have registered information, you must make several decisions. It is not always appropriate to share what you have noted as intuition. You must gauge the value of doing so for your client. The first decision may be what it is that you do with the information. The therapists in the Charles (2004) study confirmed that sometimes it is appropriate to verbally share the information with your clients. For example, you may say, "I have a sense that maybe you don't really want to take that promotion." You offer the observation tentatively, giving the client a great deal of room to reject the insight. You might not verbally share the insight but instead engage in some action based on the information. For example, you may steer the conversation in a seemingly tangential direction. Finally, you can choose to hold onto the information. You may file it in the back of your mind for a host of reasons.

One of the reasons you may choose not to share the information is because you are unsure of its validity or accuracy. Intuition, or what feels like intuition, has been noted by therapists in a number of studies to be less than 100% accurate (Charles, 2004; Stickle & Arnd-Caddigan, 2019; Witteman et al., 2012). You must validate what you think you have learned. Participants in the Charles (2004) study noted that one strategy they used to do so was to be explicit about having had an insight, or sense, or feeling, and asked their client if it was accurate. As noted previously, you may choose to act on the insight you have intuitively gained. If you do so, you must keep in mind that the information could be wrong. You must move slowly, and carefully assess your client's response from moment-to-moment. If the treatment moves forward, if your client gains new insights or opens up to a new area of exploration, or accesses an important memory, you may conclude that your intuition was accurate. Another cue to the accuracy of intuition that was identified by the Charles (2004) study participants is when the same insight arrives repeatedly.

Besides the accuracy of the information, your choice to share or not share must be based on the client's comfort level with work on this level. Sharing intuitive insights with your client may be welcomed by the client or experienced as intrusive. The therapists in the Charles (2004) study indicated that clients may respond in positive ways, such as feeling reassured, or using the insight as a spring-board to greater self-disclosure, or gaining new awareness, insights, or understanding. When they react in this way, you may interpret the forward movement as an indication that future disclosures of intuition may be welcome. Clients may alternatively have a negative reaction to the shared insight, including employing defenses or engaging in avoidance behaviors. In some cases, the client may have a mixed reaction, or not have any apparent reaction to the therapist using his/her intuitively derived knowledge in a session.

The Charles study did not offer advice on what to do when your client reacts negatively, or with ambivalence, or does not overtly react to your intuitive insight or the action you take as a result of such an insight. If you note either ambivalence or a negative reaction to your use of intuition, it is incumbent on you to blinker any further information you may glean from this source. You must also take time to repair any breaches in the therapeutic alliance, and work with sensitivity and appropriate timing on defenses and avoidance. This final recommendation circles back to the extra-therapeutic activity of engaging in education, training, supervision, and/or consultation with a therapist who is experienced in using clinical intuition.

Applying this ability to the clinical context requires that you engage in the practices and develop the personal characteristics associated with general intuition practices. In addition, you have the added responsibility to use them in a professional setting with the understanding that you are employing this ability solely for the benefit and well-being of your client. In order to do so, you must nurture the following capacities:

Clinical Intuition

Develop your self-awareness.

Regulate your own needs, desires, and expectations.

Know and apply formal theory.

Gather information relevant to the case from multiple sources.

Establish a connection with your client.

Cultivate openness and receptivity.

Ground and center if you become overwhelmed.

Note all subtle and passing qualia.

Center on your client.

Surrender to the process.

Gauge your client's comfort level with intuition; do not share if it is not welcome.

Gauge the value of the information you've gained intuitively for your client; do not share if it is not helpful.

Validate the information you have gained. Be humble and remember that it may not be accurate.

---

1. Clinical intuition requires a very high level of *self-awareness*. This is necessary to spot your projections, countertransference, and confirmation biases that may muddy your intuition, as well as the ability to "catch" the subtle subjective experiences that are the harbingers of intuitive information. This level of self-awareness can be developed through meditation, training therapy, consultation, and/or working with a group focused on developing and using clinical intuition.

2. Besides noting your reactions, you must have the ability to *regulate your own needs, desires, and expectations*. This will also serve in enhancing the likelihood of intuition being accurate, and help you avoid projecting your own processes onto the client.

3. Clinical intuition can be enhanced by a thorough knowledge of *theory and formal education*. You cannot leave your professional training at the

door. There is a distinct difference between an intuitive person and a therapist.

4. Along the same lines, you cannot disregard all of the resources you have available to you. *Gather as much explicit information as possible*, be that records, testing results, history, and paralinguistic behaviors in the room with your client.

5. Engage in some kind of symbolic/imaginal activity to help you establish a *connection* between your client and yourself.

6. *Cultivate a sense of openness and receptivity* to what you can experience that may concern your client.

7. You may choose to engage in an *in vivo* exercise to *ground and center* yourself when you begin to feel overwhelmed or swamped by your client's material or feelings.

8. *Note all of the qualia* that arise in you during the session, and ask yourself what it may mean or indicate, or if it is relevant to your client's situation.

9. *Center on your client*: attend to them with the desire to know what it's like to be them. Absorb yourself in their experience.

10. It takes a great deal of effort to center on your client so closely while simultaneously being highly aware of passing qualia within yourself. Ironically, the ability to maintain this binocular view is the result of *surrendering*. This may seem counterintuitive, but you will develop the feel for this as you practice intuitive inquiry.

11. *Gauge your client's comfort level with work on this level*. If working on this level will feel intrusive, unwelcome, or promote any kind of discomfort in your client, you are well advised to engage on a more surface level until sufficient trust has been established.

12. You must *gauge the value of sharing the information with your client*. There will be many times when you will simply want to hold on to a feeling or sense.

13. If you choose to share with your client, do not tell them with great authority what you know. *Check to see if your intuition is accurate*. You can be wrong, and you need to be ever mindful of this fact.

All of these methods can help you in the process of intuitive inquiry, to which we turn now.

7.2 Intuitive Inquiry

Perhaps the *sine qua non* of "talk therapy" is the process of engaging your client in dialogue. This dialogue often is structured around you asking your client questions. In Interpersonal Psychoanalysis this process is termed "detailed inquiry" (Sullivan, 1970). In the Intersubjective School, there is a similar process called "sustained empathic inquiry" (Stolorow, 1994a, 1994b).

Detailed inquiry is aimed at the goal of drawing attention to, and ultimately opening, the loops of meaning that keep clients locked in difficulty. It is the process of asking questions, not only, or even primarily, for the purpose of gaining information. Rather, the main intention is to draw the client's attention to patterned mental processes (Cooper, 1995/2015). The questions revolve around the client's actual past experiences with important people, because Interpersonal Analysis is premised on the assumption that it is actual interpersonal experience that forms personality. Thus, when the past is the focus of detailed inquiry, it is not assessment but an intervention in that it helps the client gain insight into their patterned interpersonal interactions while simultaneously developing a therapeutic relationship with the analyst. Detailed inquiry is also aimed at everyday experiences in the here-and-now, again, with the aim of helping the client and therapist develop a therapeutic relationship while drawing the client's attention to patterned ways of experiencing self-with-other.

The process unfolds in a sequence: the therapist asks questions, draws inferences about the client based on the answers, and then shares those inferences with the client. The therapist must be willing to reject their own ideas when they are not endorsed by the client and/or if there is not additional clinical material to support the view. In other words, the therapist is not an expert and does not know more about the client than the latter knows about themselves. In addition, the therapist is advised to generate alternative explanations for the same material. In all cases, the process moves forward by the therapist focusing on selectively inattended material.

Selectively inattended material encompasses the aspects of experience that are not elaborated on by the client. Very much in keeping with the Freudian idea of the defense of repression, selective inattention is the process in which experiences that trigger discomfort are excluded from awareness. In the process of asking questions, the therapist continues to delve into the places that the client glosses over or avoids. Again, not in an effort to "show" the client something that the therapist has already determined about the former but rather in the spirit of mutual exploration and discovery.

Detailed inquiry is based on the premise that what can be known about another person can only be known through language (Stern, 1995/2015). Interpersonal Analysis is in direct opposition to the more Freudian notions of "nonverbal unconscious communication in clinical psychoanalysis—in concepts like communication from one unconscious to another, projective identification, containment, affect attunement, and empathy" (Stern, 1995/2015,

p. 107). Sullivan (1954/1970) was clear that overt forms of communication, including words and gestures, were the only means by which private experience could be shared. And this process is fraught because we share words without necessarily sharing meanings. Thus, we can think we know what someone is attempting to communicate and be entirely wrong.

Detailed inquiry focuses the therapist's attention on what is not said: the "gaps and inconsistencies in the patient's verbal presentation" (Stern, 1995/2015, p. 108). This perspective is in stark contrast to the theory that supports MCDT. As discussed in Chapters 1 and 2, a mind-centered depth approach is premised on the understanding that mind is directly sharable, and it is the sharing of mind that supports not only understanding the client but is mutative as well.

Sustained empathic inquiry is a feature of the Intersubjective School of Psychoanalysis (Stolorow, 1994a, 1994b). Like detailed inquiry, this method is also an investigatory stance that is aimed at understanding the subjective experience of the analysand. This includes the latter's subjective experience of the analyst and the analytic encounter. "What's it like for you to be with me, here, now?" It is "an attitude that consistently seeks to comprehend the meaning of a patient's expressions from a perspective within, rather than outside, the patient's own subjective frame of reference" (Stolorow, 1994a, p. 44). It is aimed at "investigating and illuminating the principles that *unconsciously* organize a patient's experiences. Such unconscious principles become manifest, for example, in the invariant *meanings* that the analyst's qualities and activities recurrently come to acquire for the patient" (Stolorow, 1994a, p. 45, italics in original). Again, in as is the case with detailed inquiry, the process opens the client to reflection on their mental processes, contents, and states:

> Sustained empathic inquiry by the analyst contributes to the creation of a therapeutic situation in which the patient increasingly comes to believe that his most profound emotional states and needs can be understood in depth. This, in turn, encourages the patient to develop and expand his own capacity for self-reflection and to persist in articulating ever more vulnerable and sequestered regions of his subjective life.
>
> (Stolorow, 1994b, p. 148)

In other words, the process is aimed at facilitating "the unfolding, illumination, and transformation of the patient's subjective world" (Stolorow et al., 1995, p. 10).

Geist (2007), from a self-psychological/Intersubjective Perspective, discussed a variation of sustained empathic inquiry which he calls sustained empathic immersion. Sustained empathic immersion is a way of "listening and responding . . . rooted in an unwavering empathic stance" (Geist, 2007, p. 3). This stance is comprised of three overlapping approaches to empathic listening. The first is vicarious introspection, in keeping with the work of Heinze Kohut's definition of empathy. In this form of empathetic listening, the analyst aligns their subjective experience with the patient's in order to feel, within themselves, some of the subjective experiences (motivations, fears, expectations, etc.) of the patient. Interestingly, Geist cites many of the forms of intuition identified in the literature on both general intuition and clinical intuition as a way of knowing what the patient is experiencing. These include associations, affective states, and images. Geist observed that "analysts rely on vicarious introspection when we are less sure of our understanding of the patient or when we are coming to know new aspects of the patient" (2007, p. 10).

The second form of empathy Geist (2007) identified is empathic resonance. In this form of empathic engagement, there are fewer questions but a more unselfconscious, spontaneous, playful give-and-take between the analyst and the patient. Both are immersed empathically in the other's subjectivity.

The third mode of empathic listening identified by Geist (2007) is somatic empathy. For Geist (2007), physical feelings that arise in relation to a patient "reflect a visceral communication . . . [of] memories that occurred previous to our capacity for symbolization and is outside the realm of verbal expression . . . [that] take the form of enacted communication" (2007, p. 12). Again, it must be noted that these kinds of somatic experiences were cited by the therapists in the Stickle and Arnd-Caddigan study (2019) as a form of intuition. In all three of these empathic modes, Geist has suggested that the therapist is able to enter into a mutual connection with the client, and, through unconscious communication, is able to share to some degree the client's subjective experiences that represent both here-and-now experiences as well as past experiences that continue to exert a pull on the here-and-now.

Geist (2007) was clear that shifting between these three modes of empathy is more therapeutically advantageous than shifting between theoretical formulations. He suggested that remaining in an empathetic stance rather than interacting from a theoretical agenda builds the therapeutic alliance, contributes to the client's development of the capacity for therapeutic change, and helps the analyst know how to respond to the patient according to their unique needs and the moment-to-moment dynamics of an on-going therapy.

We see here that in both detailed inquiry and sustained empathic inquiry/immersion, the process is one in which the therapist brings an attitude of curiosity to the subjective world of the client. Whereas in detailed inquiry the vehicle for understanding is language, in sustained empathic inquiry/ immersion there is a recognition that the therapist can come to know (always, to a limited degree) the subjectivity of the client. Geist (2007) described in his understanding of sustained empathic immersion the way that the therapist uses intuition in order to guide the unfolding of the therapeutic process in response to the shifting needs of each unique client. This is precisely what the therapists in the Stickle and Arnd-Caddigan (2019) study identified as the therapeutic value of clinical intuition.

While what the therapist can know is an important aspect of both detailed inquiry and sustained empathic inquiry, what is even more important is that the process helps the client gain insight into their patterns or the organizing principles of their experiences. By sharing these patterns with the analyst, the possibility to open them up expands. Cosmopsychism and MCDT explain why/how the act of sharing is mutative: extended mind, or coupled oscillators, allows the client's mind to assume some of the therapist's greater mental cohesiveness, complexity, and flexibility.

Intuitive inquiry is one-part detailed inquiry, one part sustained empathic inquiry/immersion, and a double dose of clinical intuition. A mind-centered depth approach to therapy, as was described in Chapter 1, is based on the epistemological position (the view of how one can know about reality) that intuition is a legitimate, appropriate, and perhaps the only way one can know the mind aspect of reality. Thus, not surprisingly, intuition emerges as an important element in MCDT. Intuition is an important guide in determining how you respond to what your client just said or did, including their paralinguistic behaviors.

Intuition, however, transcends the role of a means to know what the client may be experiencing and how they are responding to treatment. Because intuition requires a connection between the minds of the therapist and the client, it has mutative properties. In this way, it becomes the primary tool used in the intervention process of helping clients change their minds. The principle MCDT "technique" is intuitive inquiry.

Like both detailed inquiry and sustained empathic inquiry, the therapist is an active participant in an unfolding process of supporting the client's increasing awareness of relatively inflexible patterns of perceiving and interpreting experiences. Unlike detailed inquiry, we assume that the therapist and client are able to understand each other on a very deep, non-verbal level.

Intuitive inquiry is a highly individualized process, which cannot be manualized. Indeed, any kind of map to show the path of intuitive inquiry is likely to make one miss the most breathtaking vistas. There is, however, one general guideline that may be helpful in the process: pay attention to that which the client tends to gloss over or avoid—the selectively inattended. Pay attention to that which is not being said. Not with the belief that the therapist already knows what is to be found there but with a sense of mutual curiosity and discovery. In the unfolding of this dialogue, you rarely change the subject. The material that your client produces is like a rope, made of several twined strands. You pick up on one of those strands to go deeper into your client's experience, not wider into a variety of experiences. Additionally, you must be willing, in the course of this dialogue, to change your mind and give up any theories you may hold about your client.

To an even greater degree than sustained empathic inquiry, non-verbal forms of communication are a bedrock for intuitive inquiry. Indeed, it is your intuition, which is a function of the connection between you and your client, that leads the way in the inquiry process. You inspect your subjective experiences, allowing awareness of qualia to well up, and understanding that they may carry important information about the client and/or the treatment process. You have honed the ability to discern whether these qualia are endogenous or exogenous, but never assume that you know the client's mind. You always check your intuition in the ways that were noted previously. Because intuition requires a mental connection between therapist and client as noted previously, not only does it help lead the process of discovery through greater knowing but also has its own mutative capacity.

Recall Chapter 2, where we discussed the effects of minds extending and blending in a therapeutic field. Tronick and his associates' (1998) dyadically expanded states of consciousness hypothesis, the Boston Change Process Study Group's (2010) work, and Galatzer-Levy's (2009) analogy with coupled oscillators all predict that when a therapist's and client's minds are connected in a manner that fosters clinical intuition, the shared consciousness adds information, cohesion, and complexity to both minds. Thus, intuitive inquiry encompasses all three areas of clinical change action: it fosters insight, it requires a new kind of relational experience, and it directly impacts the minds of the client and the therapist.

Intuitive inquiry is an offer for a connection that cannot be forced. It begins with the question, "What is it like to be this client?" We attempt to narrow in on answers to this question, not to further assess or plan treatment. Not to inform an objective, or satisfy our curiosity, or try to lead the client to a different ("healthier") experience. Rather, we attempt to enter into what it's like to be this client, first, so that they can begin to elaborate on what it's like to be themselves. As they represent their experiences in language, they gain a perspective on parts of their involvements and interactions that they have not previously experienced. Secondly, as we center on our clients in a consistent, curious, respectful, non-judgmental, authentic way, we offer them a relationship that they may not have been offered or able to accept previously. They feel how important they are to us and can count on being safe at all times. They can relax, assured that they will not be shamed, humiliated, or harshly judged. Third, if and when it is safe for our client, we enter into a shared space. When their qualia are shared, they become more complex, coherent, and flexible. The client is freed to experience in a new way, as old patterns are disrupted.

7.3 Conclusion

The application of general intuition to the clinical context requires that you always place your fiduciary responsibility to the client front and center in your activity. Intuition is never 100% reliable. It most often runs awry when the individual projects their own needs, desires, fears, or patterned ways of experiencing onto a situation. In order to help mitigate these propensities, it is incumbent on the intuitive therapist to cultivate as much self-awareness and the ability to self-regulate as possible.

As a professional, you must use the resources available to all therapists. This includes grounding in formal theory, the use of collateral information, and the ability to blend both discursive, logical problem solving with more associative, creative, intuitive thought.

In session with your client, you can create a connection with your client by a variety of means. You can ground and center in order to refrain from being highjacked while entering your client's experiences. You note the qualia that you experience, and check in a variety of ways to ensure that these qualia are providing useful, accurate information. Even as you focus on your qualia, you maintain a focus on your client. This split focus can often be aided by an attitude of surrender to the therapeutic field.

You must also make a professional judgment concerning whether or not you want to share what you intuitively discover with your client. There are a variety of reasons and circumstance why you may wish to refrain from doing so. Always, always, always, your judgment is based on your client's needs and ability to profitably use what you learn. Having these aspects of clinical intuition in mind, you engage in intuitive inquiry. This is the process of exploring what it's like to be your client through dialogue. By using your intuition in the unfolding of the interaction, you will help your client activate the three mutative aspects of MCDT.

7.4 Key Points

- Clinical intuition is a special application of general intuition. You have a professional, fiduciary responsibility to use your intuition in a way that will protect your client's best interests, autonomy, and self-determination.
- Because clinical intuition carries this additional responsibility, and because the therapist's projection is the dominant means by which intuition goes wrong, you have a special responsibility to take actions to increase your self-awareness and your ability to self-regulate.
- You must also use all of the professional tools available to you as a therapist in conjunction with your intuition. Intuition does not replace sound therapeutic practice, it enhances it.
- In session, you can engage in a number of practices to help you access intuition.
- You use your intuition to guide the process of intuitive inquiry, which is a way of engaging your client to accomplish the three mutative aspects of therapy: a means of developing insight to change rigid patterns, a new kind of relationship that contributes to new patterns, and a connection of minds that helps the client become more flexible.

7.5 References

Arnd-Caddigan, M. (2019). Clinical intuition and the non-material: An argument for dual-aspect monism. *Journal of Religion and Spirituality in Social Work, 38*(3), 281–295.

Bion, W. R. (1965/2015). Memory and desire. In C. Mawson (Ed.), *Three papers by W. R. Bion* (pp. 1–10). Routledge.

Boston Change Process Study Group. (2010). *Change in psychotherapy: A unifying paradigm*. W. W. Norton & Co.

Charles, R. (2004). *Intuition in psychotherapy and counselling*. Whurr.

Cooper, A. (1995/2015). The detailed inquiry. In M. Lionells, J. Fiscalini, C. H. Mann, & D. B. Stern (Eds.), *Handbook of interpersonal psychoanalysis* (pp. 679–694). Routledge.

Freud, S. (1912). Recommendations to physicians practicing psycho-analysis. In J. Strachey (Ed. & Trans.), *The standard edition of the complete psychological works of Sigmund Freud* (Vol. 12, pp. 109–144). Hogarth Press.

Galatzer-Levy, R. M. (2009). Good vibrations: Analytic process as coupled oscillations. *International Journal of Psychoanalysis, 99*, 983–1007. https://doi.org/10.1111/j.1745-8315.2009.00188.x

Geist, R. (2007). Who are you, who am I, and where are we going: Sustained empathic immersion in the opening phase of psychoanalytic treatment. *International Journal of Psychoanalytic Self Psychology, 2*(1), 1–26.

Geller, S. M., & Greenburg, L. S. (2012). *Therapeutic presence: A mindful approach to effective therapy*. American Psychological Association.

Petitmengin-Peugeot, C. (1999). The intuitive experience. *Journal of Consciousness Studies, 6*(2–3), 43–77.

Stickle, M., & Arnd-Caddigan, M. (2019). *Clinical intuition: From research to practice*. Routledge.

Stern, D. B. (1995/2015). The detailed inquiry. In M. Lionells, J. Fiscalini, C. H. Mann, & D. B. Stern (Eds.), *Handbook of interpersonal psychoanalysis* (pp. 79–138). Routledge.

Stolorow, R. D. (1994a). The nature and therapeutic action of psychoanalytic interpretation. In R. Stolorow, G. Atwood, & B. Brandchaft (Eds.), *The intersubjective perspective* (pp. 43–55). Rowman & Littlefield.

Stolorow, R. D. (1994b). Converting psychotherapy to psychoanalysis. In R. Stolorow, G. Atwood, & B. Brandchaft (Eds.), *The intersubjective perspective* (pp. 145–154). Rowman & Littlefield.

Stolorow, R. D., Brandchaff, B., & Atwood, G. E. (1995). *Psychoanalytic treatment: An intersubjective approach*. The Analytic Press.

Sullivan, H. S. (1954/1970). *The psychiatric interview: A guide for therapists and other interviewers, by the founder of the interpersonal theory of psychiatry*. W. W. Norton & Co.

Tronick, E. Z., Bruschweiler-Stern, N., Harrison, A. N., Lyons-Ruth, K., Morgan, A. C., Nahum, J. P., Sander, L., & Stern, D. (1998). Dyadically expanded states of consciousness and the process of therapeutic change. *Infant Mental Health Journal, 19*(3), 290–299.

Witteman, C. L. M., Spaanjaars, N. L., & Aarts, A. A. (2012). Clinical intuition in mental health care: A discussion and focus group. *Counselling Psychology Quarterly, 25*(1), 19–29.

Clients' Intuition   8

When I designed the research for *Clinical Intuition: From Research to Practice*, I was interested in learning about how and why therapists use their intuition professionally. I did not anticipate that the participants would discuss teaching their clients about intuition. Because of research design constraints, I didn't follow up on why or how they do this. But in looking at the literature on intuition, it became clear to me that teaching clients about this ability can significantly contribute to the goal and objectives of MCDT.

It's important to stress that in MCDT, we do not teach clients to access and trust their intuition for the sake of having a special ability. To be sure, there are plenty of people who value (and perhaps over-value) their intuition in order to be "special." But intuition, as we have seen throughout this book, is not extra-ordinary.

8.1 Intuition and a Mind-Centered Depth Therapy (MCDT)

Teaching clients to access and trust their intuition is a central aspect of a mind-centered depth approach to therapy. The goal of MCDT is to help clients overcome rigid patterns of experience in order to be able to live in new, more complex, enlivening ways. This means that the person is able to recognize—and appreciate—their individuality and uniqueness,

DOI: 10.4324/9781003090816-11

as well as experience themselves as connected and part of the whole. The fact that people are enminded and part of the universal whole means that when we experience the connection between the endogenous mind and the exogenous mind, we are able to enjoy an enlargement of our minds. We "know" or acquire information from the exogenous mind. This is intuition. By teaching our clients intuition, we help them expand their minds.

In the process of achieving this goal, we also address several objectives that may arise as important in the course of therapy. Remember that MCDT holds that each individual client presents with unique needs. Nonetheless, there are many issues that arise repeatedly in therapy that can be addressed by helping our clients be open to intuition.

8.2 Therapeutic Value of Becoming More Intuitive

Just as I reviewed the literature written by intuitive people on how to develop intuition, I turned to this corpus to see what they had to say about why it is useful to cultivate this capacity (see Appendix B for an annotated bibliography of the books that I analyzed). Three categories emerged from this review: benefits to the individual, benefits to relationships, and benefits to one's experience of their place in the universe.

Intuitive authors agree that developing intuition goes hand-in-hand with improvements in one's sense of self. There appears to be a reciprocal relationship between intuition and the sense of self: self-awareness is a pre-requisite for intuition and is enhanced as intuition improves. The intuitives whose books I analyzed noted the following benefits intuition brings to the sense of self:

- Enhances self-trust and self-confidence.
- Improves self-esteem.
- Increases inner direction/authenticity.
- Helps develop an appropriate sense of danger.
- Aids in goal-setting.
- Helps one perceive (and capitalize on) opportunities.
- Promotes self-healing.
- Enhances creativity.
- Helps one realize their potential.
- Improves the sense of well-being.
- Improves integration of parts of the self.

Helping clients access and trust their intuition may also contribute to improved relationships. Again, the content analysis I did on books on intuition cited the following benefits intuition confers on relationships:

- Helps improve communication.
- Aids in the ability to tune into/understand/read others better.
- Helps one set boundaries.
- Contributes to more meaningful relationships.
- Helps one become a better judge of character.

Finally, the data from the books I analyzed suggested that enhancing intuition helps people find a deeper meaning or sense of belonging. Specifically, they cited that intuition supports the sense of belonging in the universe, helps expand consciousness, and helps people perceive transpersonal dimensions of experience.

These three categories list a number of issues that we typically see as related to the problems for which our clients seek help. As we will see, teaching our clients to be open to intuition is one way we can help our clients resolve their difficulties.

8.3 Helping Clients Develop Intuition

With the benefits listed previously in mind, helping clients to access and trust their intuition may be a powerful intervention in MCDT. How do you teach your clients to improve their intuition? Chapter 6 offers a good template for helping your clients. Here is a brief summary of the template, with some added suggestions based on my own practice, for how you can bring the material into the session in order to encourage the benefits of being more intuitive that were noted previously. Some of these suggestions are just good, generic therapy. Others are more particular to MCDT and the development of intuition.

8.3.1 Introducing Intuition

As you orient your client toward their own intuition, you may wish to begin by teaching them that intuition is a natural, normal capacity that everybody— at least potentially—has (even while some people find it easier to access than others). As an instance of the universal mind, they are already connected. Normalize and de-pathologize intuition, hunches, gut feelings, etc. Help clients value their intuition and inquire if they are interested in enhancing their own intuitive capacity. Inquire about the experiences they have had that may have led them to devalue intuition and experiences in which their intuition helped them. Invite your client to bring their intuitions into the session.

8.3.2 Body Work

On one level, doing body work is a necessary pre-requisite for engaging with mind. Your client cannot focus on subtle qualia if their bodies are in discomfort. Thus, having a healthy body is foundational to reflecting on mind. You may wish to help your client build healthy habits, like eating and sleeping well. You may also wish to suggest they engage in regular physical activity.

Recall from Chapter 6 that regular physical activity is associated with improved intuitive capacity. Physical activity is also associated with additional objectives consistent with MCDT. There are two issues related to the body that the process of developing intuition through physical activity may address. First, bodies are a significant marker of value in our culture; your body's color, size, and primary and secondary sexual features influence the access you have to resources and power. For many, this means that their bodies are associated with shame and oppression. As we saw in Chapter 3, when an experience accompanies difficult qualia, or threatens the sense of self or important relationships, we often defensively cut ourselves off from reflecting on those qualia. In this way, many clients have banished qualia associated with or connected to their bodies to the realm of unwanted experience. Recall that experience on this level is often the subject of projection, which is a major contributing factor for mental difficulties.

This situation is exacerbated when the body is the site of physical abuse; dissociation often occurs, which is experienced as a separation of the body and the mind. Once again, when this happens, qualia associated with being embodied cannot reach the level of reflected experience. These individuals often cannot discern when they are hungry, or tired, or in pain (Emerson, 2015). For these clients, integrating the body and the mind means being able to reflect on qualia related to the body, or re-engaging the experience of what-it's-like to have somatic qualia.

There is another situation in which body work is very helpful. There are clients who have a relatively poor capacity to reflect on any kind of qualia. Some clients come to therapy without the ability to identify what it's like to have a very broad range of experiences. The psychoanalyst Christopher Bollas (1987) identified what he called normotic illness; he defined this state as "the numbing and eventual erasure of subjectivity in favour of a self that is conceived as a material object among other man-made products in the object world" (p. 133). He continues:

> some people have annihilated the creative element by developing an alternative mentality, one that aims to be objective, a mind that is characterized less by the psychic (by the representational symbolization of feelings, sensations, and intersubjective perceptions [mind]) than by the objective [matter]. This mentality is not determined to represent the object, but to be the echo of thingness inherent in material objects, to be a commodity object in the world of human production.
>
> (Bollas, 1987, p. 136)

In other words, Bollas's normotic person has cut themselves off from their minds, and they experience themselves and the world strictly as matter that can be viewed objectively.

The normotic person may present in therapy with an inner emptiness, numbness, or lack of joy. They may be highly successful, in part because they put their energy into doing and achieving external things. They are often highly conformative, following rules rather than being guided by an inner ethic. This person is easily noted in the consulting room, as they tend to side-step talking about themselves. In the terminology of MCDT, these are people whose minds are weakly developed or are repressed. That is, they have great difficulty reflecting on a broad range of qualia.

Because this individual is so concrete and so centered on matter, helping them awaken to qualia may be more easily achieved by beginning to do so in relation to somatic experiences. Asking someone what it's like to work for a boss who is never satisfied with their work may be much more difficult to identify than asking them what they are feeling in their chest right now. Because our culture teaches that the body and material things are real, asking a person to begin to open up to their subjectivity is (perhaps paradoxically) more easily accomplished when the subjectivity is turned on something material: their bodies.

It must be stressed that in doing body work with clients, the focus is always to encourage our clients to re-mind their bodies. That is, we help them to focus on what it's like to have certain specific physical experiences. David Emerson (2015) and Bessel van der Kolk (2014) have developed an approach to yoga that is very well suited to this type of work: Trauma-sensitive yoga (TSY). In TSY, the entire focus is on the qualia associated with various forms and movement. For example, the therapist/instructor may cue the client to see if they can feel which muscles are stretching and which are contracting during a form. Or to focus on how those muscles are changing as the client moves into or out of a form. Again, I want to stress that this attention to the body is the act of reflecting on qualia: mind. We draw our client's focus to their bodies as a way to connect to subjective experience, which is mind. This allows them, once again, to move their experience from the unformulated or unwanted to the reflective.

You may also consider guiding your client through progressive relaxation exercises. Again, these exercises are very helpful in integrating the body and the mind, as mind is drawn to specific parts of the body, to specific muscles, and to the degree of tension or relaxation in those muscles. Like TSY, this exercise helps to expand your client's repertoire of qualia to enhance the ability to reflect on both the body and the mind. This will heighten the ability to catch the subtle qualia that are the forms of intuition, and also generally expand the client's capacity to have new, different experiences.

Helping Clients Open up to Their Intuition

Introduce the concept of intuition as a normal, natural phenomenon, and explicitly invite your client to share their intuitive experiences.

Help your clients integrate the mind and the body by asking them to identify somatic qualia.

Help your client develop a sense of self as an individual. This includes working on self-concept, self-awareness, agency, and self-esteem. This process can be aided by working with the cotransference and with enactments.

Help your client develop a sense of self as connected. This includes the ability to discern the origin of qualia, as well as recognizing the impact they have on others.

Guide clients to tune in and catch qualia as they arise.

Help your clients value their character and identify and cultivate desired character traits.

Encourage your clients to engage in creative activities.

Explore dreams, fantasies, and daydreams in session.

Engage your client in active imagination.

Encourage your clients to journal intuitive experiences.

Offer intuition support groups.

8.3.3 The Self as Individual

As noted previously, there is a reciprocal, reinforcing relationship between self-work and your client's intuition: self-work is a preparatory aspect of intuition and intuition, as we have seen, contributes to a healthy sense of self. Self-work is at the core of MCDT, as it encapsulates that which is perhaps people's most comprehensive qualia: what it's like to be me. Self-work encompasses all of the qualia that are associated with the sense of self as individual. This includes self as continuous and bounded, as well as agency, self-esteem, self-concept, self-awareness, etc. Thus, self-work will be on-going, helping your client identify their repetitive patterns of perceiving and interpreting experience and differentiate intuitive insights from projections. In a reciprocal fashion, as they increase their intuitive capacity, they will overcome many debilitating patterns associated with what it's like. The mental connection necessary to use intuition will form a dyadically expanded mind; intuition both requires and enhances an open, flexible mind.

Two analytic methods that can aid in helping your client identify their repeated patterns or endogenous qualia are working with the cotransference and enactments. Transference is viewed in analytic circles as how the client perceives or experiences the therapist, based on expectations from past relationships. Countertransference is a more complicated construct, but generally refers to the ways that the therapist perceives and experiences the client. Cotransference suggests that both the client and the therapist are influencing each other, each exerting a pull on the other. Neither one is entirely distorting the other based on endogenous qualia, and likewise neither is free of their own endogenous proclivities. If my client is experiencing me as maternal, there is something about me that can realistically be interpreted as maternal, whether or not I intend for it to be construed that way. Cotransference can be illustrated by the example of combining colors: I am emitting blue into the analytic field. My client is emitting yellow. We are both taking in green: the interaction of blue and yellow. We each experience ourselves and the other in ways that are new and greater than the sum of the endogenous and exogenous experiences.

Working with the cotransference in MCDT means helping clients identify the qualia that arise in relation to interactions with the therapist, and determining which are familiar, or patterned experiences based on the client's past. Once the pattern has been identified, the client and the therapist can explore whether or not this pattern is associated with the client's suffering or dissatisfaction and what alternatives may be helpful. In order to do this work successfully, the therapist must be open to owning their contribution—intended or not—to the client's experience of them.

Enactments are situations in which the forward movement of the therapy seems to have been derailed by an interaction between the client and the therapist. The therapist usually notes, retrospectively, that the interaction feels "off" or fraught. You have a sense that you are behaving in a way that is not therapeutic, and perhaps a bit alien to you. The question once again becomes, is this familiar to the client? Is this part of their patterned way of being? The therapist must be able to accept their own role in contributing to the situation. By identifying it, and how each participant contributed, the client can simultaneously gain insight, have a new relational experience, and join with the therapist's mind in figuring out what happened and how.

8.3.4 The Self as Connected

Both cotransference and enactments occur in the therapeutic field, where both the therapist and the client are contributing to the experience. Thus, both methods of working with clients can help them identify their unhelpful rigid patterns as well as help them identify the effects that other people's minds have on them. Helping clients observe when and how they contaige other people's affect—or how their experience is a reflection of what another is experiencing—is an important part of the overall project. As we help them develop their intuition, their ability to identify the process of contaiging improves as well. As stated in Chapter 4, I have had many clients present for treatment, especially for anxiety. Upon exploration, it turns out that these clients assume others' feelings very easily but mistake them as something that they themselves are producing. Helping them learn the difference between the two is important. And learning how to deal with other people's feelings is equally important. It is a mistake to guide your clients to firm up their boundary so that they don't contaige qualia; this will cut them off from very important information. But helping them learn how to use and quickly metabolize these experiences is crucial to their well-being.

Equally important is helping clients realize and take responsibility for the impact they have on others. Intuition is a function of connectedness. Helping clients understand that they play a role in the universe means that they must take responsibility for the effects of their actions. What do others contaige from them? In doing so, they will find that they are able to engage in more mutually satisfying social relations.

8.3.5 Learning How to Catch Qualia

Guide your clients to tune in and catch passing qualia. Help them identify the forms in which it comes to them. Again, you can help them understand that internal images, sounds, sensations, affects, etc. are all important. Many clients, like many of the therapists in the Stickle and Arnd-Caddigan (2019) study, may respond to talking about feeling energy come and go, become more or less intense, and/or move through them. Some clients engage in this conversation by referencing chakras. As always, you must judge what your client is comfortable discussing, and a suitable form and vocabulary for such discussions.

Usually, people have several different forms that they experience, even while one of these forms may be dominant. It is valuable to talk about your client's inter-session experiences of intuition, as well as sitting with them and encouraging them to allow the forms of intuition in the here-and-now to arise.

8.3.6 Practicing Mindfulness and Intuitiveness in Session

It may be helpful to teach your client mindfulness practices, such as meditation or centering prayer, as a precursor to asking them to practice accessing intuition. These practices can help steady the mind, so that intuitive insights will not overwhelm your client, as well as help open their minds to new qualia.

Set aside time to help your clients practice accessing intuition in session. Have them sit comfortably, relax, ground and center, then open. Have them describe passing qualia. Ask them about images, sounds, physical and affective feelings, etc. For those who experience what they identify as energy, you can guide them to tune into energy: is it intense or subtle, is it moving or still, is it rhythmic or static-y? Prior to engaging in this form of practice, you may guide them through meditation practices, including guided meditations. It is very important that the approach to such practices you introduce to your client is consistent with their worldview/spiritual orientation, not yours.

8.3.7 Developing Character

Helping clients to identify and develop character traits that are important to them may help in enhancing their intuitive ability. Certain virtues or characteristics seem to be associated with being more intuitive. Among these are humility, honesty, kindness, understanding, and optimism. Characterological barriers to intuition include selfishness, self-delusion, ego, arrogance, fear of failure, and self-imposed limitations that arise from social conditioning and belief systems. Again, clients often present for therapy completely identified with quantitative measures: how much they weigh, how many friends they have on social media, how much money they make, etc. They may identify themselves with their bodies or physical characteristics, with demographic markers (I am working-class, I am straight, etc.), or with specific abilities like "good at writing." None of these are wrong or bad. But helping them begin to identify more with values, morals, and characterological aspirations (I would like to be more patient, I am a compassionate person, etc.) can be very helpful to their well-being, and may enhance their intuitive capacity.

8.3.8 Creative Activities

You may encourage your client to engage in creative activities and non-verbal forms of expression to stimulate associative (system 1) thinking. You might suggest they do so between sessions, or you may engage in such activities during session. You don't need to do art therapy to use creative activities in the treatment process. Crafts, like vision boards, can be very helpful.

8.3.9 Explore Dreams, Fantasies, and Daydreams

Along similar lines, you may value and explore your client's dreams, fantasies, and daydreams. Again, by doing so, you are helping them engage in the more associative, creative from of thought that some associate with intuition. Of particular note on this topic, I have repeatedly worked with people who do not report daydreams or fantasies. In some cases, as they begin to bring these experiences into the session, they report them as centered on external grat-ification, such as achieving money, status, esteem, etc. When I ask what it's like in the daydream to obtain that which is desired, they cannot elaborate. They shrug, or say, "I don't know," or simply, "good." The work then becomes one of helping the client begin to develop or catch qualia that arise first, as the client reports the dream or fantasy, and then the experiences that arose during the dream or fantasy. Thus, by helping clients engage in and reflect on dreams, daydreams, and fantasies, you are helping them to fully experience their minds (qualia), which will in turn help them open up to intuition. From a Jungian perspective, dreams and fantasies are the royal road to the uncon-scious. In helping clients develop their intuition by using this method, you are also helping them reflect on unformulated and unwanted experiences.

Very closely related to exploring dreams, fantasies, and daydreams is the Jungian practice of active imagination. It must be immediately noted that the process of active imagination for Jungians and post-Jungians far transcends accessing intuition. This is a core technique to achieve the Jungian goal of acti-vating the transcendent function and thus achieving individuation. From the perspective of MCDT, active imagination can be used to help clients gain access into and freedom from those rigid patterns of perception and interpretation.

The Jungian analyst Joan Chodorow (1997) compiled Jung's references to active imagination in a single volume. The way that this exercise unfolds was described by Jung as occurring in two steps: "First, letting the unconscious come up; and second, coming to terms with the unconscious" (Chodorow, 1997, p. 10). These two steps have been further delineated by subsequent writers. Chodorow summarized the works of von Franz (1980), Dallett (1982), and Johnson (1986). In Chodorow's summary, the three systems synthesized led to the conclusion that to access active imagination, you empty your mind and/or open up to or invite the unconscious. Next, you allow the unconscious to take a form, or choose a form/symbol to focus on. Then, you enter into a dialogue with the form or give it some other kind of expression. The Jungians hold that active imagination has a moral imperative attached to it, and thus recommend that you interrogate the values that are expressed in the experience and bring those values forward into your life. Johnson also suggests that you ritualize the process in order to make it concrete.

Jeffrey Raff (2000) has also outlined a process for active imagination. His is a seven-step method. The first stage is quieting the discursive mind. Secondly, you set an intention for a particular image or to find an answer to a specific question. Third, the image becomes animate, followed by the fourth stage, which is comprised of an interaction with the image or personification. Fifth, logic and discursive thought are brought into the process to interrogate the experience. Following this stage, there is some resolution, wherein the question is answered or the issue that initiated the exercise is resolved. Finally, there is integration, wherein the new insight is brought into one's life.

Note how close the process of initiating active imagination is to that of accessing intuition. Remember from Chapter 6 the formalized practice to allow an intuitive insight: relax, open, and note qualia. This is very similar to the Jungian description of engaging in the exercise of active imagination. In my own work with active imagination, I have found it to be a very useful method to open up to intuitive insights. I have previously researched therapists using their imagination to help them understand their clients and the therapeutic process better (Arnd-Caddigan, 2012; Arnd-Caddigan, 2013). This was before I began to understand intuition to the degree that I do today. I have come to understand that during the process of imagining, one may be able to trigger intuition. Thus, I am suggesting that the method of active imagination can be used with clients to help them access intuition.

To this end, I guide my clients in a grounding and centering practice, guide them to open up to and invite a symbolic form, and engage in dialogue, then slowly return to awareness of the room. During the process, I ask them to report on the nature of the form that they imagine. I leave it to them to share or not share the conversation, but, upon "return," I ask them if they would care to share any intuitive insights that they may have experienced. These are then subject to journaling. As is the case with so many of these exercises, one reason helping our clients access and trust intuition may be associated with their impact on bringing unconscious material into reflective awareness. By doing so, the exercises may help our clients loosen rigid patterns of perceiving and interpreting experience that may be associated with mental difficulties.

8.3.10 Journaling

Ask your client to journal intuitive experiences. This helps clients begin to see patterns in which experiences tend to be more accurate and which tend to be less accurate. Once again, this helps in the process of self-awareness, creating a recursive enforcement of self-awareness and intuition.

8.3.11 Support Groups

You may decide to create an intuition support group. This may be an opportunity for people who wish to enhance their intuition to find support and validation. In addition, the group may broaden the opportunity for the members to experience a dyadically expanded mind.

These suggestions are based on the material that has been published on intuition. It will be interesting to see what arises in the research on the topic. It is early in the process of researching the clinical use of intuition. Undoubtedly, we will learn a great deal from future studies.

8.4 Conclusion

Teaching your clients to access and trust their intuition is one of the ways that MCDT accomplishes many treatment objectives. Remember, specific treatment objectives are not prescribed in this approach to therapy; each client's experiences of what-it's-like are unique, and MCDT is targeted to those qualia that are associated with problems in living. Having said that, almost every form of therapy we know addresses the way the client relates to the self, the way that they relate to others, and what they understand to be their place in the universe. These are all areas of functioning that may improve as they become more comfortable with their own intuitive capacity.

8.5 Key Points

- The benefits of helping your clients access and trust intuition may be associated with improvements in their sense of self, their relationships, and their sense of their place in the universe.
- Helping your clients develop their intuition can be accomplished by using the template developed in Chapter 5 on developing your own intuition. This includes helping clients with both the preparatory practices as well as engaging in direct practices in the session, or assigning exercises as homework for your client.
- The template for opening intuition is very similar to Jung's method of active imagination. It must be noted that for Jungians, this method has benefits far beyond accessing intuition.

8.6 References

Arnd-Caddigan, M. (2012). Imagining the other: The influence of imagined conversations on the treatment process. *American Journal of Psychotherapy, 66*(4), 331–348.

Arnd-Caddigan, M. (2013). Imagined conversations and negative countertransference. *Journal of Psychotherapy Integration, 23*(2), 146–157.

Bollas, C. (1987). *The shadow of the object: Psychoanalysis of the unthought known.* Columbia University Press.

Chodorow, J. (1997). *Encountering Jung: Jung on active imagination.* Princeton University Press.

Dallett, J. (1982). Active imagination in practice. In M. Stein (Ed.), *Jungian analysis* (pp. 173–191). Open Court.

Emerson, D. (2015). *Trauma-sensitive yoga in therapy: Bringing the body into treatment.* W. W. Norton & Co.

Johnson, R. A. (1986). *Inner work: Using dreams and active imagination for personal growth.* Harper & Row.

Raff, J. (2000). *Jung and the alchemical imagination.* Nicolas-Hays.

Stickle, M., & Arnd-Caddigan, M. (2019). *Clinical intuition: From research to practice.* Routledge.

van der Kolk, B. (2014). *The body keeps the score: Brain, mind, and body in the healing of trauma.* Penguin Books.

von Franz, M. (1980). Supplement: On active imagination. In M. F. Keyes (Ed.), *Inward journey: Art as therapy* (pp. 125–133). Open Court.

Witteman, C. L. M., Spaanjaars, N. L., & Aarts, A. A. (2012). Clinical intuition in mental health care: A discussion and focus group. *Counselling Psychology Quarterly, 25*(1), 19–29.

Conclusion: Metaphysics and Psychotherapy

Psychotherapy is the process of helping people change their minds. We know that it takes a great deal of vulnerability—and hence bravery—for a client to engage in this process. It may well be time for us therapists to take inspiration from our clients and change our minds. Perhaps we can change our minds regarding the very nature of mind, its relationship to the body, and its place and value in the universe.

Changing mind is a function of opening your mind. We must recognize the fact that each of our minds is a relatively stable pattern, and hence is unique. Over-focus on this individuality has clearly not led to well-being. We are naïve to think that if we keep focusing on the same thing, that we will have a new outcome. We can change our view to acknowledge that the twin states of consistency in experience (boundedness) and the ability to experience novelty (permeability) are the balance that is associated with optimal human mental functioning. We know this already. What we do, and what we have always done, is open our clients to new ways of experiencing in order to find contentment.

Robin Brown (2020) in *Groundwork for a Transpersonal Psychoanalysis* has suggested that psychoanalytic theory and practice would benefit from taking a panpsychic, participatory turn. In doing so, he is quite clear that psychoanalysis has historically endorsed a metaphysical perspective even while denying that they were doing so. We know well what happens when we repress or deny things: they leak out in unexpected ways. And what has leaked out in psychoanalytic theory, indeed, most theories of psychotherapy, is materialist reductionism. The field is replete with examples of the supposition that mind is either reified or a side effect of neurochemical processes.

DOI: 10.4324/9781003090816-12

Materialism has certainly led to many advances in civilization. Medicine and technology have expanded our life-expectancy and made the lives of most humans more physically comfortable than that of our predecessors. And so, it is important that as we interrogate the hegemony of this worldview, we don't throw the baby out with the bathwater. Science is the best way to help us understand the material aspect of reality.

But science has not solved all of our problems. Indeed, a lopsided view of the world that only admits the reality of matter has brought us great pain. We are materialists in both senses of the term; it is not only the dominant ontology but we also value the acquisition of stuff. We are ranked in terms of how much stuff we have. This consumerism has fueled an ecological crisis. And it has contributed to a mental health crisis and a social crisis.

Perhaps it is precisely because of the pain associated with failing to recognize the mental aspect of the universe that philosophers are once again asserting the reality of mind. Their position has much to offer the field of mental health. How can we possibly move toward better psychotherapeutic treatment if we ultimately don't believe that mind is real? How does psychotherapy change if we recognize that mind is a real, fundamental, and omnipresent aspect of the universe?

One result of this move is that it situates humans in the context of a greater whole. It recognizes that we are not islands of individuality. We form a vast network of seemingly individual minds that are, in actuality, instantiations of the singular mind. We cannot not impact the world around us. This places great responsibility on each of us to use our minds wisely. This gives us even greater motivation to provide for the mental well-being of others.

If we adopt this metaphysical position, there are important implications for how we conduct psychotherapy—the process of helping minds change. In spite of the fact that our minds are ontologically connected, we can create situations in which we fail to honor that connection. When adult minds fail to offer mental connections with infants, the young mind cannot grow, expand, and develop complexity. Just as there is a possibility of a lack of connection (unformulated experience), adults can engage in a form of mental connection that is threatening (unwelcome experience). These experiences block the child's ability to symbolize and reflect on the qualia engendered by and/or associated with those experiences. That which cannot be reflected on is doomed to be continuously re-lived. The individual continually perceives and interprets new situations as if they are that which the individual cannot reflect upon. Or the adult's failure to hold the child's mind in their mind leaves the child swamped with exogenus qualia, unable to discern the source of the experience. Because they misattribute the source, they are unable to appropriately metabolize the experiences.

There is also the possibility for a connection that is grounded in understanding, support, respect, and validation. This connection allows a mind to risk openness, to admit new experience, to change. This is at the very heart of a mind-centered depth approach to therapy. In MCDT, we help our clients overcome the debilitating effects of early unsuccessful connections with other minds. In connecting, we help them loosen rigid patterns of perceiving and interpreting experiences that were not shared or were met with disapproval. This work supports changes in our clients' minds on several levels. We use interpretation and deconstruction to help clients alter what-it's-like to experience situations on which they are able to reflect: experiences that they are able to put into words. We help them alter the effects of experiences on which they cannot reflect, experiences that they cannot verbalize. In other words, we help clients change at the level of the "unconscious," or based on experiences that were unformulated and/or unwelcome. We do so by offering a new kind of relationship in which experiences can be safely shared. We also help our clients by using our direct mental connection with them to dyadically expand their minds in order to admit new experiences. These can include experiences that our clients may never have even imagined.

We help our clients expand their ways of experiencing by helping them focus on the dual aspects of humanity. These are our individual, unique being and our connectedness to the whole. Our connectedness means that our self-boundaries, while extant, are also permeable. Our clients may benefit from work on both aspects. That is, we can help our clients enhance their awareness of their relatively stable ways of perceiving and interpreting their existence; we can help them develop their self-esteem such that they can recognize and take pride in their strengths, even as they are able to discern and accept their imperfections. We can help them realize that they are agents, capable of making choices and affecting the world around them. We also help them feel their connectedness, including their place in a larger scheme, and the ways that they are affected by—and affect—exogenus forms of mind.

The connection between our mind and our client's mind is a pathway for communication of important information. This is intuition. It is not some strange occult phenomenon. It is something that we have been doing since we were born. It is the way humans develop. We know this. Infant development research has demonstrated repeatedly that human minds connect, and information is shared in this state. Several different forms of psychotherapy have recognized the importance of intuition to the human being as well as to the therapy process. Different psychoanalytic schools have recognized the role of communication between minds and have chosen to apply a number of different words to this process. Perhaps it is time to reduce the stigma and own the word "intuition."

If we are going to work with our clients by using our intuition, we must develop this ability in a general sense. Given that it is normal and natural, the need to develop the capacity may be a function of the degree to which one has suppressed it due to cultural constraints. Once we have reconnected to our intuition, we can begin to apply it to the clinical context.

The professional application of our intuition carries special constraints. As a fiduciary relationship, we must be very clear why we are using our intuition and the effect that it is having on our client and the therapeutic process. This means that we must be ever mindful that what feels like intuition can be the projection of our own wishes for our clients, or our own unacknowledged issues. We cannot share or act on any insight until we have validated it. Likewise, we must be clear that any intuitive insight we might have will be valuable to the client and the therapeutic process. Finally, we must not use intuition if our client is uncomfortable with this process. When we have erred, as is inevitable, we must repair the therapeutic alliance, and learn from our mistakes.

Intuition can be used clinically in the process of intuitive inquiry. This is a process of dialogue with our clients wherein we encourage our clients to delve deeper and deeper into the experience of what-it's-like. This spans the range of what it's like to experience their symptoms, the interpersonal dynamics they are involved in, what it's like to be in the world, and what it's like to be themselves. We do so by working to understand their experience, even as we stay centered on our own passing, subtle qualia that may carry important information about our client and about their situation.

Finally, we may teach our clients to be open to and trust their own intuition. Doing so can aid our efforts to help them develop their sense of self, help them to experience more satisfying relationships, and help them experience a sense of belonging in the world. In helping our clients develop their intuition, we may aid in the process of integrating the mind and the body. We help them with the ability to see themselves as more than the quantitative variables that are valued in our culture. They are able to reflect on experience more fully and deeply. They also can find greater comfort and safety in their bodies.

What a mind-centered depth approach to therapy helps clients develop is a full appreciation that we have dual, dual natures: we are bodies and minds; we are connected and separate. If therapy is going to contribute to our clients' global well-being, we must value the complex, multifaceted nature of humanity. Rather than being a manualized form of treatment that streamlines the decision-making process, we open therapy up to the messiness of life that is rich and meaningful. We become comfortable with uncertainty. We apply the fullness of our mental capacities to help our clients open to the fullness of theirs. To do so, we must recognize the impact of our metaphysical commitments.

Reference

Brown, R. S. (2020). *Groundwork for a transpersonal psychoanalysis: Spirituality, relationship, and participation.* Routledge.

Appendix A: Developing Intuition

Annotated Bibliography

Agor, W. H. (1989). The logic of intuition: How top executives make important decisions. W. H. Agor, Ed. *Intuition in organizations: Leading and managing productively.* 157–170. Newbury Park, CA: Sage.
Agor cites Vaughan (see the following list).

- Value intuition and have the intention to develop it.
- Devote time to intuition and create a special space for developing it.
- Let go of physical and emotional tension.
- Learn to quiet the mind through such techniques as meditation.
- Face self-deception and be honest with yourself and others.
- Learn to be quiet and receptive.
- Tune in to both inner and outer processes.
- Produce nonverbal expressions, such as drawings or music, without a specific goal in mind.
- Trust yourself and your experience.
- Be open to all outer and inner experiences.
- Be willing to experience and confront your fears.
- Have a non-judgmental attitude toward things as they are.
- Practice love and compassion.
- Be willing to accept things as they are.
- Practice paying daily attention to intuition.
- Keep a record of intuitive insights.
- Find friends with whom you can share your intuitive experiences and who do not judge you.
- Find intrinsic satisfaction from expanded consciousness.

Ilan, C. (2019). *A little bit of intuition: An introduction to extrasensory perception.* **New York, NY: Sterling Ethos.**
This book has a very concise chapter on how to develop intuition.

- A pre-condition is a calm mind and a relaxed body. Therefore, engage in a grounding activity to calm your body and mind.
- A regular meditation practice helps not only to calm the mind but also to process [metabolize] the past.
- Observation: delve into your inner being. Releasing attachment to what is going on around you, you can observe without judgment or competing to be heard or taken seriously. This will allow you to discern patterns.
- Journaling both helps you process as well as provide you with feedback. Over time, the feedback concerning when intuition was correct and when it was not allows you to recognize a specific sensation you get when you are accurately receiving information.
- Patterns: in deeply observing yourself and events and people around you, you will open your awareness to patterns. You can choose what you want to do if you or someone else is replaying an old pattern.
- You must grant yourself permission to be right. You must stay open, and trust. You will begin to discern when energy that you feel is "yours" and when it's "not yours."

Day, L. (1996). *Practical intuition: How to harness the power of your instinct and make it work for you.* **New York, NY: Broadway Books.**
Two basic steps: gather symbolic material/impressions and then translate (turn them into a narrative).

- Relax and open.
- Attend to impressions: see, hear, feel (somatic and emotional), taste, smell, think, etc. This is a non-logical phase, not a time to try to make sense of the incoming impressions. Logic can, in fact, interfere at this stage. These are fragments. It's okay if you "make things up."
- Translate: create a narrative out of the impressions. Here, the logical, linear aspect of mind has a role. Again, it may feel like you're "making stuff up."
- Validate. Over time, you will begin to discern a different feel between real intuition and projection. Not real intuition comes from a place of attachment and aversion. A not real intuition is judgmental and is emotionally charged (p. 95).

K. [only initial of surname is given] L. (2017). *Intuition on demand: A step-by-step guide to powerful intuition you can trust.* Rochester, VT: Findhorn Press.

This book avoids any metaphysical or ontological speculation. It is exactly what it says it is: a technique.

- The technique is ABCDP:

  - Ask a question: don't ask yes/no or rhetorical questions; don't ask about something you are very emotional about. Ask an open-ended emotionally neutral question.
  - Be open: the "thinking mind" must be quiet and relaxed. Don't second-guess; don't judge. Fragments will pop-up. Don't try to prematurely make meaning out of the fragments.
  - Collect and receive: when fragments pop-up, ask another question to get more fragments rather than trying to use your thinking mind to elaborate on a fragment. It's "real" intuition when it's non-judgmental, non-emotional, short and to the point, fleeting and subtle, there's no "I" in it, and it's symbolic.
  - Do it again. Keep asking questions based on the fragments you receive. Ask for clarification/elaboration. Put the fragments together like beads on a string.
  - Practice, practice, practice. You get better at it over time.

Jamison, T. & Jamison, L. (2011). *Psychic intelligence: Tune in and discover the power of your intuition.* New York, NY: Grand Central Life & Style.

Intuition is collapsed with the "clairs:" clairvoyance, clairaudience, claircognizance, and clairsentience. "Being psychic is about paying attention" (p. 231).

- First, open your mind to the possibility that there is more than the material, linear world, i.e. a universal consciousness.
- Be sensitive to others' needs and emotions and your own inner voice (p. 30). This means don't deny what you know (p. 31).
- Be willing to change; take risks, live on the edge.
- Be authentic.
- Stop overthinking and worrying; give yourself permission to "step into your power" (p. 35).
- Don't be afraid to fail.
- Trust in yourself.
- Take care of yourself: body, mind, and spirit; slow down, set healthy boundaries, sleep, and eat properly.

- Self-discovery: examine and let go of your fears (p. 42), especially self-doubt. This means trusting something higher (p. 44).
- Cleanse your own negative energy (p. 46). And don't suck up other people's negativity (p. 55).
- Use affirmations to cement your intentions.
- Let go of behaviors, thoughts, and beliefs that don't serve you, as well as material possessions.
- Engage in creative activities (stimulate the right brain).
- (p. 65) IQ + E. I. = psychic intelligence, so raise your E. I.
- Attend to the forms of intuition (the four "clairs," or images, sounds, feelings, and thoughts). They provide exercises to practice seeing, hearing, feeling, and knowing as mental simulations (practicing in the imagination).

Margolis, C. (2008). *Discover your inner wisdom: Using intuition, logic, and common sense to make your best choice.* New York: Simon and Schuster.

1. Believe in intuition.
2. Become aware of your thoughts.
3. Discern "my" thoughts from "not my" thoughts.
4. Tune into infinite knowledge / energy.
5. Discern intuitive information from your thoughts, emotions, desires, etc.
6. Check your intuition with logic and common sense.
7. Identify and protect against negative energies.
8. Overcome barriers:

   a. Selfishness (use insights to help others).
   b. Self-delusion.
   c. Ego (cultivate gratitude).
   d. Arrogance (become a student).
   e. Fear of failure (be willing to make and recognize mistakes).
   f. Your self-imposed limitations (go beyond what you think you can do).

9. Create the right atmosphere (relax, quiet the mind).
10. Focus on the present; clear your mind of thoughts.
11. Ask a question without being emotionally involved.
12. Pay attention to what comes to you (know the forms your intuition takes).
13. Be patient.

Peirce, P. (2009). *The intuitive way: The definitive guide to increasing your awareness, new and expanded edition.* New York, NY: Atria.

This author understands intuition to be a side effect of a spiritual process. While she does not identify specifically as a Christian, there are strong Christian biases in the work.

- Cultivate a beginner's mind: listen and receive new data and be open to the unknown.
- Let go of control to be neutral and receive, align with "universal truths."
- Trust yourself, trust the process: pessimism kills intuition; needing to be positive [toxic positivity] leads to gullibility and prevents you from discriminating. You need common sense and optimism [the theme of trust is repeated].
- Detach from worries, "should," and strong opinions.
- Realize how much unconscious negativity shapes your view of life, especially attachment to security; catch yourself when a negative worldview is operating.
- Pre-conditions: honesty, kindness and understanding, and a positive attitude.
- Pre-conditions: connection-seeking; diversity-appreciating; eccentricity-enjoying, and surprise-cultivating (p. 128).
- Soften your awareness (p. 82); be patient, be content (p. 82), and have "engaged indifference" (p. 88).
- Stop the internal dialogue (p. 88).
- Be present and notice what is (p. 82).
- Listen to your internal self-talk and suspend your involvement with negativity (p. 28) [self-awareness and self-regulation].
- Become aware of your body: your "internal posture" and bodily sensations [interoception/proprioception] (p. 20). Merge your mind and body (p. 96). Bring your conscious mind into your body (p. 97).
- Identify "flow" and when it "hits a dam" and release it (p. 36).
- Look at the movement of your awareness and how it shifts cyclically (p. 41).
- First phase of the process (p. 50ff):

  - Be receptive and fertile, trust, and be aware.
  - Use your senses.
  - Be clear about what you want.
  - Allow yourself to receive energy (from spirit).

- Second phase (p. 51):

  - Stay present and alert in your body.
  - Be aware of the flow and become one with the motion.

- Third phase:

  - Practice humility.
  - Cooperate; surrender to spaciousness (p. 52).

- The process (pp. 116–117). Move down the chain of knowing:

  - Move from the mind [analytic mind] language, analysis, abstraction.
  - To associations-meanings by noting imagery/symbols; sounds; textures and impressions; tastes; smells; and emotions.
  - To physical reactions, including vibrations/resonance, urges, and other somatic reactions.

- There is a thing the author calls "superconscious guidance," which is apparently like but not identical to intuition. There are 12 steps (pp. 149–151):

  - Relax your body.
  - Become alert and aware.
  - Align (be fully present in your body at this moment).
  - Attune (to your soul).
  - Focus on your need.
  - Ask.
  - Release.
  - Allow the inflow.
  - Consciously recognize the answer.
  - Record the answer.
  - Feel gratitude.
  - Implement.

Vaughn, F. E. (1979). *Awakening Intuition*. New York, NY: Anchor Books.

Appendix: Guidelines for Awakening Intuition (pp. 203–205). This is *verbatim*.

Intention: The first requirement for consciously awakening intuition is a clear intention to do so. Intuition is already within you, but to awaken it you have to value it and *intend* to develop it.

Time: your willingness to devote time to tuning in to your intuition, making a space for its unfolding in your life, is part of valuing and developing it.

Relaxation: Letting go of physical and emotional tension gives intuition the space to enter your conscious awareness.

Silence: Intuition flourishes in silence. Learning to quiet the mind is therefore part of the training for awakening intuition. Various meditative practices are useful in learning to maintain the necessary inner silence.

Honesty: Willingness to face self-deception and to be honest with yourself and others is essential. Creating any kind of smokescreen interferes with clear vision. Giving up pretenses is a big step in awakening intuition.

Receptivity: Learning to be quiet and receptive allows intuition to unfold. Too much activity or conscious programming gets in the way of intuitive awareness that emerges when a receptive attitude is cultivated.

Sensitivity: Finely tuned sensitivity to both inner and outer processes provides more information and expands intuitive knowing. Sensitivity to energy awareness and the quality of experiences is particularly useful.

Nonverbal Play: Drawing, music, movement, clay, and other forms of nonverbal expression done in a spirit of play, rather than for the purpose of goal-oriented achievement, provide excellent channels for activating intuitive, right-hemisphere functions.

Trust: Trusting the process, trusting yourself, trusting your experience, are the keys to trusting and developing your intuition.

Openness: If you are afraid of being seen, you may close up and then be unable to see. Being open to all experiences, both inner and outer, gives intuition the space it needs to develop fully.

Courage: Fear gets in the way of direct experiences and often generates deception. Your willingness to experience and confront your fears will facilitate the expansion of intuition.

Acceptance: A nonjudgmental attitude, an acceptance of things as they are, including self-acceptance, allows intuition to function freely.

Love: Opening your heart to feelings of nonjudgmental love and compassion allows you to see into the nature of things. Emotional empathy and intuitive identification are facilitated by love and compassion.

Nonattachment: The willingness to let things be as they are, rather than trying to make them be the way you would like them to be, or the way you think they should be, allows intuition to emerge. You can see things as they are only when desires and fears are out of the way.

Daily practice: Intuitive awareness grows with daily attention. If you discount or neglect it most of the time and only want it to perform occasionally, it may not respond.

Journal keeping: Keeping a record of intuitive flashes, hunches, insights, and images that cone to mind spontaneously at any time of the day or night, can help stabilize and validate them.

Support group: Finding one, two, or more friends with whom you can share your interest in the development of intuition, as well as your successes, failure, hompes, and fears, can facilitate and accelerate the process of development. Sharing experience with someone who is willing to listen without judging or interpreting, is very useful.

Enjoyment: Following intuition does not always feel good. At times it may seem difficult and entail arduous work. At other times it may be effortless. Enjoying the creative resources of intuition is based on the intrinsic satisfaction of expanding consciousness taking responsibility for your life, and surrendering to your own true nature.

- Characteristic attitudes: unconventional and comfortable in their unconventionality . . . self-sufficient; do not base their identities on membership in social groups . . . abstract, independent, foresighted, confident, and spontaneous (p. 47).
- Anxiety and wishful thinking interfere with intuition, as does conscious mind or ego (p. 59) fear and desire interfere (p. 60) strong emotions can interfere, but strong emotional ties to some people can enhance intuition (p. 60).
- Be aware of bodily responses.
- Be aware of sensitivity to other people's vibes or vibrations of energy, which come through emotions.
- Tune into mental images or inner visions.

Appendix B: Annotated Bibliography of the Benefits of Developing Intuition

Allan, C. (2019). *A little bit of intuition: An introduction to extrasensory perception.* New York, NY: Sterling Ethos.

- Strong sense of trust in yourself (even in the face of adversity).
- Enhanced self-awareness.
- Ability to detach from a situation.
- Relationships and interpersonal interactions will change; it can help create immediate bonds with others, or warn them away.

Jamison, T. & Jamison, L. (2011). *Psychic intelligence: Tune in and discover the power of your intuition.* New York, NY: Grand Central Life & Style.

- (Implied) better emotional intelligence.
- Become happier.
- Discover your life purpose.
- Develop vibrant health.
- Make more successful decisions.
- Trust your innate guidance system.
- Attract wealth and abundance.
- Overcome your weaknesses.
- Banish your fears and release emotional blocks.
- Set healthy boundaries.
- See danger coming.
- Tune in to your higher guidance.
- Bring forth greater wisdom.

- Achieve your goals.
- Find your most authentic self.
- Create more meaningful relationships.
- Become a better judge of character.
- Read paralinguistic communications.
- Recognize opportunities.
- Make better decisions.
- Predict possible outcomes.
- Define or refine career goals.
- Sharpen your financial smarts.
- Get the edge in business situations.
- Tune in to your kids.
- Trust your dating vibes.
- Be your own love psychic.
- Attract your true mate.
- Become your most authentic self.
- Rediscover your passion.
- Reinvent yourself.

Peirce, P. (2009). *The intuitive way: The definitive guide to increasing your awareness, new and expanded edition.* New York, NY: Atria.

- Improves communication; helps in making decisions; enhances creativity; promotes self-healing; enables you to manifest what you need (p. xxvii).
- Develop new authority, new skills, and new knowledge about your life (p. xxxi).
- Know your true self.
- Greater spiritual awareness.
- Simplify your life.
- Realize your full potential.
- Things work faster, more harmoniously, more efficiently.
- Perceive the "big picture."
- Better problem solving by going beyond mechanistic thinking (p. 5) [better problem-solving comes up repeatedly].
- Improves self-confidence.
- Ability to acquire information when you need it.
- Enhances psychological maturity and physical health.
- Trust increases.
- Reduces anxiety.
- Enhances hopefulness.

- Enhances accurate awareness of surroundings.
- Inspiration increases.
- Enthusiasm expands.
- You become more happy, creative, and productive.
- Enhances satisfaction.
- Expands understanding.
- Gives you more clarity, streamlines logistics, brings a unifying worldview.
- New enjoyment.
- Greater wisdom.
- Unravel core patterns of negativity.
- You will be more authentic, more grounded in your personality, and move in harmony with the collective unconscious.

Vaughn, F. E. (1979). *Awakening Intuition.* **New York, NY: Anchor Books.**

- Improved self-esteem and sense of inner direction.
- Improved self-awareness, general awareness, self-discovery, self-knowledge.
- Enhances inner freedom, personal choices. and decisive action.
- Promotes self-transcendence.
- Improves sense of well-being and harmony with oneself and the universe.
- Helps you discover who you are (experience of cosmic consciousness) and be more familiar with the transpersonal dimensions of your experience.
- Expands consciousness to understand what is true.
- Helps with integrating parts of yourself that were formerly unfamiliar, disowned, or projected.

Index

For Product Safety Concerns and Information please contact our EU
representative GPSR@taylorandfrancis.com
Taylor & Francis Verlag GmbH, Kaufingerstraße 24, 80331 München, Germany